SECOND LANGUAGE LEARNING
DATA ANALYSIS

Second Edition

SECOND LANGUAGE LEARNING
DATA ANALYSIS

Second Edition

Susan Gass
Michigan State University

Antonella Sorace
University of Edinburgh

Larry Selinker
University of London, Birkbeck College

LAWRENCE ERLBAUM ASSOCIATES, PUBLISHERS
1999   Mahwah, New Jersey   London

Lawrence Erlbaum Associates, Inc., Publishers
10 Industrial Avenue
Mahwah, New Jersey 07430

Library of Congress Cataloging-in-Publication Data

Gass, Susan M.
    Second language learning data analysis / Susan Gass, Antonella
Sorace, Larry Selinker. -- 2nd [rev.] ed.
        p.   cm.
    Rev. ed. of: Workbook in second language acquisition / Larry
Selinker, Susan Gass. 1984.
    ISBN 0-8058-3263-7 (pbk.)
    1. Second language acquisition. 2. Language and languages--Study
and teaching. I. Sorace, Antonella. II. Selinker, Larry, 1937-
III. Selinker, Larry, 1937-   Workbook in second language
acquisition. IV. Title.
P118.2.G374 1998
418'.007--dc21   98-43393
                                                                CIP

Books published by Lawrence Erlbaum Associates are printed on acid-free paper, and
their bindings are chosen for strength and durability.

Printed in the United States of America

10 9 8 7 6 5 4 3

CONTENTS

Preface

There are many to whom we owe a debt of gratitude in the preparation of this book. First and foremost we acknowledge the publishers and authors who gave us permission to reprint data presented in their original articles.

A significant source of assistance (knowingly and unknowingly) were our colleagues. Many provided us with unpublished manuscripts, others answered questions about their methodological procedures so that we could present the data more efficiently; others were so thorough in their original data that extracting data sets was an easy process. Indeed, some (especially at the University of Edinburgh) field tested some of the problems and provided feedback on their experiences. India Plough provided behind the scenes help in numerous instances, most significantly by reading through the manuscript and making comments on an earlier draft and by collecting original data for some of the problems and for the appendices. Sabine Helling, David Mosher, Catherine Tamareille and Susana Tuero (all from Michigan State University) provided the transcriptions for the German, Japanese, French and Spanish data respectively. Jim Sumbler of Michigan State University spent many many hours providing his technical expertise in the preparation of the tapes. Ildiko Svetics, who was a TA at Michigan State University in a course where the first edition was used, provided useful criticism. We are also grateful to ZhaoHong Han for assisting Larry Selinker in the preparation of this manuscript. Finally, it is not possible to sufficiently acknowledge Catherine Fleck who worked tirelessly on this revised version for many many moons. Without the assistance of all of these individuals, this book would not have seen the light of day.

Larry Selinker and Susan Gass wrote the first workbook in the field of second language acquisition in 1984, Over the years many colleagues commented on some of the problems. Their comments resulted in major changes in the problems that were retained in this book.

Working through data analysis problems as a pedagogical tool is by no means unique to the field of second language learning. In fact, in writing this workbook, we have consulted numerous workbooks from unrelated disciplines. This was an invaluable process in that we learned not only techniques for presenting small sets of organized data, but also how to ask questions based on those data.

Finally, our gratitude to our families must be acknowledged. Because we were working at a distance, numerous visits to one another's homes were necessary. Thanks to Bob and Josh for putting the others up, for putting up with the others, and for doing all that extra cooking. Thanks also to Marco, Andrew, Carlo, and Aaron for allowing your rooms to be used, and Seth and Ethan for not minding the extra commotion in the house.

Acknowledgments

We are grateful to the following for permission to reproduce copyright material. We have tried to contact everyone concerned. If we have committed unintentional errors, please notify us for future editions.

The Acoustic Society of America and the author for an extract from J. E. Flege (1988). Factors affecting degree of perceived foreign accent in English sentences. *Journal Of The Acoustic Society Of America, 84,* 70-79; John Schumann for data from *The Pidginization Process* (1978) originally published by Newbury House; John Benjamins for an extract from S. Gass & J. Ard (1984). L2 acquisition and the ontology of language universals. In W. Rutherford (Ed.), *Second Language Acquisition and Language Universals* (pp. 33 -68); Data from E. Broselow, Nonobvious transfer: on predicting epenthesis errors, in S. Gass & L. Selinker (Eds.), *Language Transfer in Language Learning* (269-280), originally published by Newbury House (1983); Cambridge University Press for the following extracts: (1) E. Kellerman (1979). Transfer and non-transfer: Where we are now. *Studies in Second Language Acquisition, 2,* 37-57; (2) S. Gass (1986). An interactionist approach to L2 sentence interpretation. *Studies in Second Language Acquisition, 8,* 19-37; (3) S. Gass & E. Varonis (1985). Variation in native speaker speech modification to non-native speakers. *Studies in Second Language Acquisition, 7,* 37-57; (4) S. Gass & E. Varonis (1982). The comprehensibility of non-native speech. *Studies in Second Language Acquisition, 4,* 114-136; (5) A. Sheldon & W. Strange (1982). The acquisition of /r/ and /l/ by Japanese learners of English: evidence that speech production can precede speech perception. *Applied Psycholinguistics, 3,* 243-261; (6) E. Varonis & S. Gass (1985). Miscommunication in native/nonnative conversation. *Language in Society, 14,* 327-343; (7) H. Zobl (1989). Canonical typological structures and ergativity in English L2 acquisition. In S. Gass & J. Schachter (Eds.), *Linguistic Perspectives on Second Language Acquisition* (pp. 203-221); (8) A. Sorace (1993). Unaccusativity and auxiliary choice in non-native grammars of Italian and French: Asymmetries and predictable indeterminacy. *Journal of French Language Studies, 3,* 71-93; (9) L. Jones (1979). *Notions in English;* The author for an extract from P. Meara (1978). Learners' word associations in French, *Interlanguage Studies Bulletin, 3,* 192-211; Julius Gross Verlag for extracts from R. Ravem (1968). Language acquisition in a second language environment. *International Review of Applied Linguistics, 6,* 175-186; Heidi Riggenbach for data from her dissertation. Heinle and Heinle for extracts from the following: (1) B. Hawkins (1985). Is an 'appropriate response' always so appropriate? In S. Gass & C. Madden *(Eds.), Input in second language acquisition* (pp. 162-178); (2) E. Kellerman, T. Ammerlaan, T. Bongaerts & N. Poulisse (1990). System and hierarchy in L2 compensatory strategies. In R. C. Scarcella, E. S. Andersen, & S. D. Krashen (Eds.), *Developing Communicative Competence in a second language* (pp. 163-178); Hodder & Stoughton for extracts from the following: (1) S. Gass & U. Lakshmanan (1991). Accounting for interlanguage subject pronouns. *Second Language Research, 7,* 181-203; (2) J. Schachter (1990). On the issue of completeness in second language acquisition. *Second Language Research, 6,* 193-124; (3) A. Sorace (1993). Incomplete vs. divergent representations of unaccusativity in non-native grammars. *Second Language Research, 9,* 22-48; (4) L. White (1991). Adverb placement in second language acquisition: Some effects of positive and negative evidence in the classroom. *Second Language Research, 7,* 133-161. The author for an extract from E. Kellerman (1986). An eye for an eye: Crosslinguistic constraints on the development of the L2 lexicon. In E. Kellerman & M. Sharwood Smith (Eds.), *Crosslinguistic influence in second language acquisition.* Oxford: Pergamon; The Linguistic Society of America for an extract from R. Coppieters (1987). Competence differences between native and non-native speakers. *Language, 63(3),* 544-573; Oxford University Press for the following: (1) E. Varonis & S. Gass (1985). Nonnative/nonnative conversations: A model for negotiation of meaning. *Applied Linguistics, 6,* 71-90; (2) E. Tarone & G. Yule (1989). *Focus on the learner; Language Learning* for extracts from the following: (1) F. Eckman (1981). On the naturalness of interlanguage phonological rules. *Language Learning, 31,* 195-216; (2) K. Hakuta (1974). Prefabricated patterns and the emergence of structure in second language learning. *Language Learning, 24,* 287-297; Basil Blackwell for an extract from E. Bialystok (1990), *Communication Strategies.*

Introduction

The purpose of this Workbook is to provide students with practice in analyzing second language data. Our intention is that this book be used by people in a range of second language courses, including practical courses concerned with second language learning and teaching as well as theoretical ones concerned primarily with acquisition as a reflection of cognitive aspects of language. We also intend that this Workbook be used as a supplement along with an introductory textbook in second language acquisition and/or with a course pack of readings in the field selected by the individual teacher.

Courses in second language acquisition serve a range of purposes—many are designed for those who are primarily interested in training future language teachers; others are designed for those who are interested in acquisition for what it can tell us about the nature of the human mind; still others tend to incorporate both of these needs and interests. Nonetheless, all have in common the need to understand what drives the learning process.

We hold to the credo that, for the student of second language learning, "hands-on" experience with actual second language data is essential in understanding the processes involved in learning a second language. That is, by working through exemplars of the kinds of interlanguages that learners do and do not create, a clearer understanding of the principles underlying these interlanguages comes about. Our goal in this Workbook is to present data organized in such a way that by working through pedagogically organized data-sets, students are led to a discovery of theoretical and/or methodological issues. In addition, they are led to the point of being able to interpret data and being able to begin to draw conclusions from them.

Generalizing from data, of course, has limitations. This is the case not only in dealing with data presented in this Workbook, but is also true when dealing with data from actual empirical studies. Teaching students to understand limitations of dealing with actual data involves crucial pedagogical lessons. In each case, we present a limited amount of data to illustrate a particular point. After an analysis of the data, more data are then presented that may either support or refute initial conclusions. Students are asked to create an account that fits the data at hand and that goes beyond the data to predict what future data might look like. It is not sufficient for students to come up with a statement that "more data are needed." Rather, that statement should be couched within a clear theoretical framework. We believe that students should go from the data to some conclusion that leads to a statement that has basically three parts: a) what else you would like to know about these data; b) why this, specifically, and not something else; and c) how one can empirically research what you want to find out. This sequence of questions force students to constantly keep in mind the important question of falsification: What kind of data would it take to falsify the particular conclusions the student has come to?

The data analysis problems in this Workbook are ultimately concerned with underlying *principles* of learning, independent of particular languages and interlanguages. Even though most of the problems in this book deal with English, we do not intend this Workbook to be used only by those interested in the teaching and/or learning of English as an additional language. To the contrary, we believe that because the book is concerned with principles of learning, these problems have as much relevance for students interested in, for example, the learning of Spanish, French, Japanese, or any other language. To take a concrete example, one problem deals with the issue of word associations in a second language (English speakers learning French). The underlying principles discovered in working through this problem relate to the organization of the mental lexicon in general, not just that of English learners of French.

In addition to the problems themselves, audio tapes are available through instructors. There are two parts to the audio tape: The first part is to be used as an accompaniment to some of the problems, the second part consists of additional data that can be used for analysis. The first part provides a richness to the problem not available through written data (those problems that have taped material are indicated by an ☺), in some instances allowing original data to be replicated; in other cases it allows access to phonetic and phonological aspects of interlanguages that cannot be discerned through transcripts alone. In the second part of the audio tape are data sets unrelated to specific problems. The data in this part are designed for students who are interested in the teaching and learning of languages other than English providing them with ample opportunities for interlanguage analyses of the language of interest.

Finally, a short glossary is provided to ensure that students have the necessary background to do the problems in this book.

The problems in this Workbook have been drawn from several sources, most notably the published literature and unpublished manuscripts. In addition, there are some problems that come from our own and/or colleagues' unpublished research materials.

We hope that we have succeeded in providing students with a representative sample of the major principles of our field and that working through these data sets will prove enjoyable as well as intellectually rewarding.

Antonella Sorace
Susan Gass
Larry Selinker

Edinburgh, Scotland

SECTION ONE

Research Methodology

PROBLEM 1.1

ACCEPTABILITY JUDGMENTS

=== **Part One** ===

For each of the following pairs of sentences, decide which of the two is more acceptable. Write the number 1 in the box next to the more acceptable sentence, and 2 in the box next to the less acceptable sentence. If the sentences are equally acceptable, write 1 in both boxes.

1.   We didn't dare answer him back.
      We dared not answer him back.

2.   We didn't dare to answer him back.
      We didn't dare answer him back.

3.   We didn't dare to answer him back.
      We dared not answer him back.

=== **Part Two** ===

For this exercise you will hear 24 sentences. If you think the sentence is correct, put an X in the box in the left-hand column marked "correct." If you think the sentence is incorrect, put an X in the box in the column marked "incorrect." If you cannot decide, put an X in the box in the column marked "not sure."

You will have approximately 5 seconds to record your answer; there will be no time for second thoughts.

1.	correct		incorrect		not sure	
2.	correct		incorrect		not sure	
3.	correct		incorrect		not sure	
4.	correct		incorrect		not sure	
5.	correct		incorrect		not sure	
6.	correct		incorrect		not sure	
7.	correct		incorrect		not sure	
8.	correct		incorrect		not sure	
9.	correct		incorrect		not sure	
10.	correct		incorrect		not sure	
11.	correct		incorrect		not sure	
12.	correct		incorrect		not sure	
13.	correct		incorrect		not sure	
14.	correct		incorrect		not sure	
15.	correct		incorrect		not sure	
16.	correct		incorrect		not sure	
17.	correct		incorrect		not sure	
18.	correct		incorrect		not sure	
19.	correct		incorrect		not sure	
20.	correct		incorrect		not sure	
21.	correct		incorrect		not sure	
22.	correct		incorrect		not sure	
23.	correct		incorrect		not sure	
24.	correct		incorrect		not sure	

=========   **Part Three**   =========

In this exercise you will rank six sentences in order of acceptability. First, decide which of the sentences is most correct and natural for you, and write the number 1 in the box next to that sentence. Then decide which of the remaining five sentences is most correct and natural, and give that sentence a 2. Continue in this way, so that you rank order the sentences from the most correct and natural to the least correct and natural. If you can find no differences in the acceptability of two or more sentences, you can give them the same number.

1. a. The letter was sent him this morning.
    b. The accident was reported him.
    c. The window was opened her.
    d. A new car was bought me.
    e. Permission to go was refused me.
    f. The door was painted them.

2. a. I was given the book.
    b. They were prepared the tickets.
    c. They were explained the problem.
    d. He was baked a cake.
    e. I was cleaned the car.
    f. She was promised a new bicycle.

3. a. What did Paul think entered the computer system last week?
    b. What did the policeman say he thought John agreed would prove his innocence?
    c. What did the policeman say he thought the thieves agreed they would steal first?
    d. What did the doctor say she suspected the patient had taken?
    e. What did the nurse say he thought would happen to the patient?
    f. What did Sarah think Lisa bought for my birthday?

4. a. Who did Hank suspect Lisa liked?
    b. Who did you say you thought the nurse reported the doctor had seen last week?
    c. Who did you say John suspects fell in love with Sue?
    d. Who did Hank suspect liked Lisa?
    e. Who did you say Bob thought Sue suspected would go to the dance with Mark?
    f. Who did the President say he thinks he'll appoint as ambassador?

=========   **Part Four**   =========

Record the scores of the whole class for Part One in the boxes below by counting the number of members of the class who gave each sentence a 1 and the number who gave that sentence a 2. Leave out those who gave equal numbers to the sentences.

		1	2
1.	We didn't dare answer him back.		
	We dared not answer him back.		
2.	We didn't dare to answer him back.		
	We didn't dare answer him back.		
3.	We didn't dare to answer him back.		
	We dared not answer him back.		

QUESTIONS

Work in small groups.

1.   Consider the recorded scores to the sentences in Part Four (taken from Part One) Compare the score that a sentence received the first time it appeared with the score it received the second time. Are there differences? If so, how do you account for the difference?

We didn't dare answer him back. (Group 1)
We didn't dare answer him back. (Group 2)

We dared not answer him back. (Group 1)
We dared not answer him back. (Group 3)

We didn't dare to answer him back. (Group 2)
We didn't dare to answer him back. (Group 3)

2.   What conclusions can you draw about the validity of this method of eliciting acceptability judgments?

3.   Record the scores of your group for Parts Two and Three and calculate the mean score/rank for each set of sentences. Compare the rank orders obtained by rating (Part Two) and ranking methods (Part Three). (Use Worksheets at the end of problem).

    a.   Are the rank orders obtained by the two methods the same or different for each of the four items? If so, account for these differences.

    b.   What difference would it have made to your responses to Part Two if there had only been two categories, "correct" and "incorrect"?

    c.   What are the advantages and disadvantages of the two methods used in Parts Two and Three (rating and ranking)?

WORKSHEET FOR RATING EXERCISE

Code responses as follows: "Correct" = 2; "Incorrect" = 0; "Not sure" = 1. **Numbers in left margin represent order on tape.** After you have calculated the means, rank the sentences in each item from most acceptable (1), to least acceptable (6).

Item 1

JUDGES

	A	B	C	D	E	Sum	Mean	Rank
7 — The letter was sent him this morning.								
3 — The accident was reported him.								
11 — The window was opened her.								
24 — A new car was bought me.								
19 — Permission to go was refused me.								
9 — The door was painted them.								

Item 2

JUDGES

	A	B	C	D	E	Sum	Mean	Rank
21 — I was given the book.								
6 — They were prepared the tickets.								
12 — They were explained the problem.								
18 — He was baked a cake.								
4 — I was cleaned the car.								
1 — She was promised a new bicycle.								

Item 3

JUDGES

	A	B	C	D	E	Sum	Mean	Rank
20 — What did Paul think entered the computer system last week?								
5 — What did the policeman say he thought John agreed would prove his innocence?								
2 — What did the policeman say he thought the thieves agreed they would steal first?								
10 — What did the doctor say she suspected the patient had taken?								
13 — What did the nurse say he thought would happen to the patient?								
16 — What did Sarah think Lisa bought for my birthday?								

Item 4

JUDGES

	A	B	C	D	E	Sum	Mean	Rank
17 — Who did Hank suspect Lisa liked?								
22 — Who did you say you thought the nurse reported the doctor had seen last week?								
23 — Who did you say John suspects fell in love with Sue?								
14 — Who did Hank suspect liked Lisa?								
15 — Who did you say Bob thought Sue suspected would go to the dance with Mark?								
8 — Who did the President say he thinks he'll appoint as ambassador?								

WORKSHEET FOR RANKING EXERCISE

Item 1

The letter was sent him this morning.
The accident was reported him.
The window was opened her.
A new car was bought me.
Permission to go was refused me.
The door was painted them.

JUDGES							
A	B	C	D	E	Sum	Mean	Rank

Item 2

I was given the book.
They were prepared the tickets.
They were explained the problem.
He was baked a cake.
I was cleaned the car.
She was promised a new bicycle.

JUDGES							
A	B	C	D	E	Sum	Mean	Rank

Item 3

What did Paul think entered the computer system last week?
What did the policeman say he thought John agreed would prove his innocence?
What did the policeman say he thought the thieves agreed they would steal first?
What did the doctor say she suspected the patient had taken?
What did the nurse say he thought would happen to the patient?
What did Sarah think Lisa bought for my birthday?

JUDGES							
A	B	C	D	E	Sum	Mean	Rank

Item 4

Who did Hank suspect Lisa liked?
Who did you say you thought the nurse reported the doctor had seen last week?
Who did you say John suspects fell in love with Sue?
Who did Hank suspect liked Lisa?
Who did you say Bob thought Sue suspected would go to the dance with Mark?
Who did the President say he thinks he'll appoint as ambassador?

JUDGES							
A	B	C	D	E	Sum	Mean	Rank

═══ PROBLEM 1.2 ═══

RELATIVE CLAUSES

Native Language: Japanese, Thai, Farsi, Portuguese
Target Language: English
Data Source: Sentence combining & acceptability judgments
Learner Information:
      Age: Adults
      Learning Environment: Students in an ESL program, U.S.
      Proficiency Level: High intermediate to advanced
      Number of Subjects: 5

THEORETICAL BACKGROUND

Relative clauses can be ordered in what is known as the Accessibility Hierarchy (Keenan & Comrie, 1977, Noun phrase accessibility and Universal Grammar, *Linguistic Inquiry,* 8, 63-99). The basic principle is that one can predict the types of relative clauses a given language will have based on the following hierarchy:

ACCESSIBILITY HIERARCHY

SU   >   DO   >   IO   >   GEN >   OCOMP

Subject relative clause:
    That's the man [<u>who</u> ran away]. (*who* is the subject of its clause)

Direct object relative clause:
    That's the man [<u>whom</u> I saw yesterday] (*whom* is the direct object of its clause)

Indirect object relative clause:
    That's the man [*to whom* I gave the letter]

Genitive relative clause:
    That's the man [*whose sister* I know].

Object of comparative:
    That's the man [*whom* I am taller than].

Two claims are important here: First, all languages have subject relative clauses and second, predictions can be made such that if a language has a relative clause of type X, then it will also have any relative clause type higher on the hierarchy, or to the left of type X. Thus, if we know that a language has object of preposition relatives (*That's the woman about whom I told you.*), we know that it also has subject, direct object, and indirect object relatives. There is no *a priori* way to predict the lowest relative clause type. But when the lowest type is known, we are able to make claims about all other relative clause types that that language has.

METHODOLOGICAL BACKGROUND

Sentence Combining: Subjects were told to combine two sentences using a relative clause. They were told to begin with the FIRST sentence.
Acceptability Judgment: Subjects were asked to judge whether sentences were good English sentences or not good English sentences.

==========   **Part One**   ==========

The following are the sentences used in the sentence combining task.

Sentences:

1.	The boy fell.	The boy's girlfriend left him.
2.	The girl laughed.	The boy is bigger than the girl.
3.	The girl laughed.	The boy gave the girl a book.
4.	I saw the girl.	The boy gave the girl a book.
5.	The girl slept.	The boy hit the girl.
6.	I saw the girl.	The boy is bigger than the girl.
7.	I saw the girl.	The boy hit the girl.
8.	I saw the man.	The man came.
9.	I saw the boy.	The boy's girlfriend left him.
10.	The man fell.	The man came.

The data below are from five learners of English on the sentence combining task.

Learner 1
Native Language = Japanese

1. The boy whose girlfriend left him fell.
2. The boy is bigger than the girl who laughed.
3. It girl whom the boy gave a book laughed.
4. I saw the girl whom the boy gave a book.
5. The boy hit the girl who slept.
6. The boy is bigger than the girl who I saw.
7. The boy hit the girl who I saw.
8. I saw the man who came.
9. I saw the boy whose girlfriend left him.
10. The man who came fell.

Learner 2
Native Language = Farsi

1. blank
2. The girl laughed at the boy who is bigger than her.
3. The girl laughed at the boy who gave her a book.
4. I saw the girl whom the boy gave her a book.
5. The boy hit the girl who slept.
6. I saw the girl who is smaller than the boy.
7. I saw the girl whom was hit by the boy.
8. I saw the man who came.
9. I saw the boy's girlfriend who left him.
10. The man who fell came.

Learner 3
Native Language = Thai

1. The boy fell then the boy's girlfriend left him.
2. The girl laughed at the boy who is bigger than her.
3. The girl laughed while the boy gave her a book.

4.   I saw the girl whom the boy gave her a book.
5.   The boy hit the girl who slept.
6.   I saw the girl who the boy is bigger than her.
7.   I saw the girl whom the boy hit.
8.   I saw the man who came.
9.   I saw the boy who his girlfriend left him.
10.   The man who came is fallen.

Learner 4
Native Language = Portuguese

1.   The boy fell that his girlfriend left him.
2.   The girl laughed who is bigger than him.
3.   The girl laughed who gave her a book.
4.   I saw the girl whose book were given by the boy.
5.   The boy hit the girl who slept.
6.   I saw the girl who is bigger than the boy.
7.   I saw the girl who was hitted by the boy.
8.   I saw the man who came.
9.   I saw the boy whose girlfriend left him.
10.   The man who fell came.

Learner 5
Native Language = Thai

1.   The boy whom his girlfriend left him fell.
2.   The boy is bigger than the girl who laughed.
3.   The boy gave a book to a laughing girl.
4.   The girl whom I saw got the boy's book.
5.   The boy hit the girl while she was sleeping.
6.   The girl whom I saw is smaller than the boy.
7.   I saw the girl who was hit by the boy.
8.   I saw the man who came.
9.   I saw the boy whose girlfriend left him.
10.   The man who fell came.

QUESTIONS

1.   Categorize each of the pairs of sentences according to the type of relative clause that is being targeted.

2.   Mark those sentences in which there were learner errors. (Recall that instructions stated that they were to form a relative clause, beginning with the first sentence. They were explicitly told not to use words such as, *because, until, before*, etc.)

3.   How do the student errors relate to the Accessibility Hierarchy [SU > DO > IO > GEN > OCOMP]?

4.   Determine to what extent learners avoided producing the targeted relative clause. How do you determine avoidance in this case?

5.   For those sentence types that were avoided, what means were used to create relative clauses (other grammatical structures, word changes, etc.)?

6.   For those sentences that were avoided, what was the resultant relative clause type? How does this information relate to information about the Accessibility Hierarchy?

Part Two

The following data are from the same learners as in Part One.   These data, however, are from acceptability judgments of sentences with relative clauses.

Learner 1

		Response
1.	The woman whose brother ran away came.	Good
2.	The boy that the girl is smarter than ran away.	Not Good
3.	The teacher that she gave the book to is my sister.	Good
4.	The boy saw the woman that she loved the child.	Good
5.	The baby that was crying was hungry.	Good
6.	The man whom the woman saw left the city.	Good
7.	I saw the girl that the boy hit her.	Not Good
8.	I saw the girl that her brother ran away.	Good
9.	I saw the girl that the boy is taller than her.	Good
10.	I saw the girl that the boy gave her a book.	Not Good

Learner 2

		Response
1.	The woman whose brother ran away came.	Not Good
2.	The boy that the girl is smarter than ran away.	Not Good
3.	The teacher that she gave the book to is my sister.	Not Good
4.	The boy saw the woman that she loved the child.	Good
5.	The baby that was crying was hungry.	Good
6.	The man whom the woman saw left the city.	Not Good
7.	I saw the girl that the boy hit her.	Good
8.	I saw the girl that her brother ran away.	Not Good
9.	I saw the girl that the boy is taller than her.	Not Good
10.	I saw the girl that the boy gave her a book.	Not Good

Learner 3

		Response
1.	The woman whose brother ran away came.	Not Good
2.	The boy that the girl is smarter than ran away.	Good
3.	The teacher that she gave the book to is my sister.	Not Good
4.	The boy saw the woman that she loved the child.	Not Good
5.	The baby that was crying was hungry.	Not Good
6.	The man whom the woman saw left the city.	Good
7.	I saw the girl that the boy hit her.	Good
8.	I saw the girl that her brother ran away.	Good
9.	I saw the girl that the boy is taller than her.	Good
10.	I saw the girl that the boy gave her a book.	Good

Learner 4

                                                                              Response

1.	The woman whose brother ran away came.	Not Good
2.	The boy that the girl is smarter than ran away.	Not Good
3.	The teacher that she gave the book to is my sister.	Not Good
4.	The boy saw the woman that she loved the child.	Not Good
5.	The baby that was crying was hungry.	Good
6.	The man whom the woman saw left the city.	Good
7.	I saw the girl that the boy hit her.	Not Good
8.	I saw the girl that her brother ran away.	Not Good
9.	I saw the girl that the boy is taller than her.	Not Good
10.	I saw the girl that the boy gave her a book.	Not Good

Learner 5

                                                                              Response

1.	The woman whose brother ran away came.	Not Good
2.	The boy that the girl is smarter than ran away.	Not Good
3.	The teacher that she gave the book to is my sister.	Not Good
4.	The boy saw the woman that she loved the child.	Not Good
5.	The baby that was crying was hungry.	Not Good
6.	The man whom the woman saw left the city.	Good
7.	I saw the girl that the boy hit her.	Not Good
8.	I saw the girl that her brother ran away.	Not Good
9.	I saw the girl that the boy is taller than her.	Not Good
10.	I saw the girl that the boy gave her a book.	Not Good

QUESTIONS

7.   Categorize each of these sentences according to the relative clause type it illustrates.

8.   For each learner, determine error patterns according to relative clause type.

9.   For each learner, compare the responses on the two data elicitation measures. Do both of these elicitation measures give a similar picture of learners' knowledge of relative clauses?

10.   What information can be obtained on the sentence combining task that cannot be obtained using an acceptability judgment task?

11.   What information can be obtained on the acceptability judgment task that cannot be obtained using a sentence combining task?

PROBLEM 1.3

MISUNDERSTANDING 1

Native Language: Spanish
Target Language: English
Data Source: Two NS and NNS pairs playing "Grab Bag" Game and follow-up retrospective data

Learner Information:
      Age: Adults
      Length of Exposure
      to TL: Average 3 years
      Learning Environment: Informal exposure

METHODOLOGICAL BACKGROUND

In the Grab Bag game there was a bag containing common objects (e.g., a key, a plastic knife, a piece of gum). One member of the pair drew an item from the bag, not letting his/her partner see the object. The other person then had to discover the identity of the object by asking questions about it (Part One, Primary Data).

The retrospective data in Part Two were collected after the Grab Bag Game. The tapes of the original conversations were played back to the subjects; they were told to "stop the recorder at any time and comment on what you were thinking at that point in the conversation." The investigator also stopped the recorder and asked questions of the subjects when specific information was desired. The retrospective data were also tape recorded, which made them Secondary Data.

=========== **Part One** ===========

PRIMARY DATA

Excerpt One: (NNS knows what the item is.)

    NS: Does it make a noise?
    NNS: Noise (softly)
    NS: Noise (softly)
    NNS: No...No (softly)
    NS: No. Uhm, is it sharp?

Excerpt Two: (NNS knows what the item is.)

    NS: Hm, is it, uhm, is it made out of metal?
    NNS: Metal,...no.

Excerpt Three: (NS knows what the item is.)

    NS: Yeah!...yeah! You can...ask me like, for an idea, you know, to make it more easy.
    NNS: Uh huh
    NS: So, go ahead. Say, "What's it for?" You ask me, "What's it for?"
    NNS: What this for?

Excerpt Four: (NNS knows what the item is.)

    NS: No. Uhm, is it sharp?
    NNS: Sharp? No.
    NS: Is it uhm,...is it smooth?
    NNS: /smu/
    NS: Smooth (gestures)
    NNS: Yes

Excerpt Five: (NS knows what the item is.)

NS: Okay, uhm,...you, uhm...when you eat you use it.
NNS: Uh...hm...spoon?
NS: No...close!
NNS: Close.
NS: What else do you eat with?
NNS: Yes, but I don't know.
NS: Ah!
NNS: The name.
NS: when you cut
NNS: Yes, but I don't know the name (laughs)
NS: (laughs)
NNS: Yes!
NS: You don't know the name?
NNS: No.
NS: OK...you give up?
NNS: Yes.
NS: OK...it's a knife.
NNS: The knife.

Excerpt Six: (NNS knows what the item is.)

NS: Okay, little guy! yeah, yours! Okay! yours is it for eat?
NNS: Eat. No.

QUESTIONS

Part One, PRIMARY DATA:

1.   What evidence does the nonnative speaker provide to indicate that comprehension has taken place? Consider, in particular, the appropriateness of the responses.

2.   What does the native speaker do to help in the facilitation of comprehension?

3.   Concentrate on the repetitions in these data and complete the following chart:

REPETITION   FUNCTION

Noise (Excerpt 1-NNS)   Comprehension
Noise (Excerpt 1-NS)   Conversational solidarity

================   **Part Two**   ================

SECONDARY DATA

Retrospective Comments (RES=Researcher)

Excerpt One:

NNS: Noise-that I didn't understand.
RES: Why did you say "no" if you didn't understand the word?
NNS: Because I thought that she wouldn't be able to explain. There are some words-it's rare
        that a person can explain them.
NS: I didn't think she understood "noise."
RES: Why do you think she said "no" then?
NS: Just to be safe. But I really don't think she understood.

RES: Why didn't you pursue it then?
NS: Hmmm. I don't know.

Excerpt Two:

NNS: I didn't understand it, "metal."
NS: I thought she understood it (metal).

Excerpt Three:

NNS: I understood "you ask me," but not "idea."
RES: Did you understand all that-to make it more easy for you?
NNS: No, I didn't understand it.
NNS: He (the NS) told me to tell him what I had. He said to me "What is it that you have?"
NS: Well, he just didn't have the language or know what to ask-on anything, he had no idea what to ask. So-I also forgot he could ask for what it's for a clue about it, so I just said, "Ask me what it's for and then I'll tell you."
RES: So he asked you what it's for. Do you think he understood then?
NS: Yes.

Excerpt Four:

NNS: "Sharp" means "touched."
NNS: (after RES explains meaning) I should have listened in a different way.
NNS: (re: smooth) something soft and "shaggy."
NS: I did an audiovisual thing.

Excerpt Five:

NNS: I understood "clothes." I thought she meant something made of cloth. So, I was thinking of "tablecloth" and I didn't know how to say it.
NS: (re: "close") I think because I gave her a positive response, she knew it was nearer to the right answer. But the word I'm not sure she understood.
NNS: I was thinking of "tablecloth," but I didn't know the word in English.
NNS: (re: cut) Like if I had "captured" what she said; if I was sure.
NS: I just thought she couldn't think of the word. She knew it was a knife, but couldn't think of it.
NNS: (re: give up) I wasn't real sure of the whole sentence, but, yes, I knew what she meant. There are some things it's not necessary to know real well. You understand from all the words together. I supposed she was telling me this-she'd take the thing out of the bag and I'd tell her it.
RES: When she showed you the knife, what did you think?
NNS: I could never guess what that was what it was.
RES: Did you know how to say "knife" in English?
NNS: Yes.

Excerpt Six:

RES: Did you understand the word "eat" this time?
NNS: "For eat." No, I didn't understand it.

QUESTIONS

Part Two, SECONDARY DATA:

4.   Compare the retrospective data with the actual spoken data of Part One. Given these retrospective comments, what conclusions can you draw about the appropriateness of responses in conversations as indicators of comprehension?

5.   Given the retrospective data, describe what happens when misunderstandings occur.

6.   What kind of additional information do retrospective data add to an understanding of actual learner behavior in interactions?

SECTION TWO

The Lexicon

POLYSEMOUS WORDS

Part One

Native Language:	Dutch
Target Language:	English
Data Source:	Judgments of translatability into English of the Dutch word *breken* "break".
Learner Information:	
Age:	Adults. University students of English in The Netherlands
Length of Exposure to TL:	First- and third-year university students
Number of Subjects:	81

METHODOLOGICAL BACKGROUND

Native speaking Dutch students of English were asked to indicate which of the meanings of *breken* they would translate by the English word *break*. Below are the Dutch sentences used and the percentage of students who responded that each sentence was translatable.

Dutch Sentences (all grammatical in Dutch)	%
1. Welk land heeft de wapenstilstand **gebroken**? (Which country has **broken** the ceasefire?)	28
2. Zij **brak** 't wereldrecord. (She **broke** the world record.)	51
3. Zij **brak** zijn hart. (She **broke** his heart.)	79
4. De golven **braken** op de rotsen. (The waves **broke** on the rock.)	35
5. Hij **brak** zijn woord. (He **broke** his word.)	60
6. Hij **brak** zijn been. (He **broke** his leg.)	81
7. Het ondergrondse verzet werd **gebroken**. (The underground resistance was **broken**.)	22
8. Dankzij 'n paar grapjes was 't ijs eindelijk **gebroken**. (Thanks to a few jokes, the ice was finally **broken**.)	33
9. 'n Spelletje zou de middag enigszins **breken**. (A game would **break** up the afternoon a bit.)	11
10. Zijn val werd door 'n boom **gebroken**. (His fall was **broken** by a tree.)	17
11. 't Kopje **brak**. (The cup **broke**.)	64
12. Nood **breekt** wet. (Necessity **breaks** law—a saying)	34
13. Sommige arbeiders hebben de staking **gebroken**. (Some workers have **broken** the strike.)	9
14. Na 't ongeluk is hij 'n **gebroken** man geworden. (After the accident, he was a **broken** man.)	61
15. Zijn stem **brak** toen hij 13 was.(His voice **broke** when he was 13.)	17
16. De man **brak** zijn eed. (The man **broke** his oath.)	47
17. De lichtstralen **breken** in het water. (The light rays **break** [refract] in the water.)	25

QUESTIONS

1.   Consider the percentage of acceptance for each sentence. Order the sentences in terms of greater to lesser translatability of the Dutch word *breken,* as perceived by the students.

2.   Consider the English translation equivalents given alongside the Dutch sentences on the preceding page. Given the meanings of these Dutch sentences, what differences are there which might account for the varying degrees of translatability ascribed to them? For example, how do you account for 81% acceptance for item 6, 79% acceptance for item 3, but only 64% acceptance for item 11?

3.   How might your analysis predict the translatability of the equivalent of *break* in your native language or in another language that you know?

===========   **Part Two**   ===========

Native Language: Dutch
Data Source: Preference judgments of translatability into English
                                                  of the Dutch word *oog* "eye"
Learner Information:
     Age: Adults. University students of English in The
                                                  Netherlands
     Number of Subjects: 35

METHODOLOGICAL BACKGROUND

Students were shown sentences in pairs. Each of the sentences had a different meaning of the word *oog*. They were asked to select which meaning of *oog* they thought would be more likely to be rendered by *eye* in English.

QUESTIONS

4.   Think about the word *eye* in English or in another language you know well. How many meanings can you think of? Based on your analysis in Part One, what do you predict the relative order of translatability of these various meanings to be?

5.   Consider the data below on Dutch meanings of *oog* (eye) and the data in the following table.

Het menselijk **oog**.	The human **eye**.
Het **oog** van een aardappel.	The **eye** of a potato.
Een electronisch **oog**.	An electronic **eye**.
De **ogen** op een pauwestaart.	The **eyes** on a peacock's tail.
Het **oog** van een naald.	The **eye** of a needle.
De **ogen** op een dobbelsteen.	The spots (dots, pips) on dice.

Preference scores

	potato	peacock	electronic	human	dice	needle
potato	-----	6	0	0	10	3
peacock	29	-----	11	0	22	14
electronic	35	24	-----	1	32	24
human	35	35	34	-----	35	34
dice	25	13	3	0	----	7
needle	32	21	11	1	28	-----

This table is to be read as follows: If you look at the intersection of Column 2 and Row 1, you will see the number 6. This means that 6 people found *oog van een aardappel* (eye of the potato) more likely to be translated by *eye* than *oog op een pauwestaart* (eyes on a peacock's tail) would be. Twenty-nine people thought otherwise (6 + 29 = 35 subjects). Another example: Look at the intersection of Column 6 and Row 3. The number 24 means that 24 people thought that *een electronisch oog* (electronic eye) was more likely to be translated by English *eye* than *het oog van een naald* (the eye of a needle) would be.

6.   Order these data to reflect the relative translatability of these meanings of the Dutch word *eye* and provide an explanation for the relative ordering that you established. What features of the meanings of these words might be responsible for this ordering?

7.   Are the results from Part Two consistent with the results from Part One? If so, why? If not, why not?

8.   What conclusions can you draw on the basis of these data concerning the role of the native language in the acquisition of lexical meaning in an L2?

METAPHORS AND APHORISMS

Native Language: As noted
Target Language: English
Data Source: Observed errors from a variety of sources
Learner Information:
      Age: Adults
      Proficiency Level: Advanced

Part One

DATA

1. NNS: When you are in Rome, you must do what Romans do. (Japanese)
Suggested target form: When in Rome, do as the Romans do.

2. NNS: She regularly shoots herself in her foot. (Indian)
Suggested target form: She regularly shoots herself in the foot.

3. NNS: I woke up fresh as daisy. (KiKongo/Lingala)
Suggested target form: I woke up fresh as a daisy.

4. NNS: He is going to talk an ear off you tonight. (Spanish)
Suggested target form: He is going to talk your ear off tonight.

5. NNS: To victor belong spoils. (Russian)
Suggested target form: To the victor belong the spoils.

6. NNS: Britain has a lot of stakes in the world, the Dutch have not. (Dutch)
Suggested target form: Britain has a great stake in the world, the Dutch have not. (American: do not)

7. NNS: I will be on your cases about this one. (Dutch)
Suggested target form: I will be on your case about this one.

8. NNS: No man is island. (Indian)
Suggested target form: No man is an island.

9. NNS: That was a very good chance for us to turn the table. (Korean)
Suggested target form: That was a very good chance for us to turn the tables. (on him/her/them).

10. NNS: You can't have cake and eat it. (French)
Suggested target form: You can't have your cake and eat it too.

11. NNS: Take the monkey out our backs. (Spanish)
Suggested target form: Take the monkey off our backs.

12. NNS: If he does not observe, he will have egg on face. (Japanese)
Suggested target form: If he doesn't watch it, he'll have egg on his face.

13. NNS: A student named X gave me her list of questions, which came to her mind when she was attending the class. (Chinese)
Suggested target form: A student named X gave me her list of questions, which came to mind when she was attending class.

14.NNS: He will need something to save his face. (Russian)
Suggested target form: He will need something to save face.

15. NNS: We must give the benefit of our doubt. (Romanian)
Suggested target form: We must give him/her/them the benefit of the doubt.

16. NNS: If I'm the only one who likes it, then be it.(Dutch)
Suggested target form: If I'm the only one who likes it, then so be it.

17. NNS: I'm putting myself in her feet. (Spanish)
Suggested target form: I'm putting myself in her shoes.

18. NNS: We all have bee in the bonnet. (Indian)
Suggested target form: We all have bees in our bonnet.

19. NNS: We won't take it to lie down. (Italian)
Suggested target form: We won't take it lying down.

20. NNS: They keep on to move the goal posts on us. (Italian)
Suggested target form: They keep on moving the goal posts on us.

QUESTIONS

1. In the preceding data, consider each interlanguage form, which approximates a native speaker version. For each example, provide a more literal paraphrase. For instance, *She regularly shoots herself in the foot* might more literally mean: *She regularly sabotages herself,* and *When in Rome, do as the Romans do* might more literally mean: *One should accommodate oneself to local customs.*

2. Consider the preceding nonnative versions. In each instance the nonnative speaker modifies the original target language version. Describe the nature of the modifications made. What uniform explanation can you provide to account for the nature of the modifications made? Is one possible?

3. Describe the effect that the non-native phrasing can have on native speakers. Would this be for native speakers only?

*4. What do these data suggest about the acquisition of fixed phrases and fixed expressions?

*5. Compare each of these, either the form or the literal meaning, with such phrases in other languages you know. Do you find each of these forms/meaning in that language? Where you find differences, what sorts are they?

PROBLEM 2.3

WORD ASSOCIATIONS

Native Language: English
Target Language: French
Data Source: Word associations
Learner Information:
    Age: 16
    Learning Environment: London comprehensive school
    Proficiency Level: High intermediate
    Number of Subjects: 76

METHODOLOGICAL BACKGROUND

Learners were given a list of 100 words and were asked to write down beside each one the first French word that it made them think of.

Part One

The following table reports each of the stimulus words (Column 1), the most common native speaker response (Column 3) [French] and the most common nonnative speaker response (Column 5) [English]. English glosses are given in Columns 2, 4, and 6 (no glosses are given when they are identical to French native speaker responses). The number in the last Column indicates the number of students (nonnative speakers of French) who gave that response. Symbols preceding the learner responses represent:

=   Primary responses that are the same as the primary responses of native French speakers.
:   Words that are not the usual primary responses of native French speakers, but that do nevertheless occur in the list of their normal responses.
/   Responses that are not normally produced by native French speakers.

	STIMULUS		NS RESPONSE		NNS RESPONSE		#
1.	table	*table*	chaise	*chair*	=chaise		53
2.	sombre	*dark*	clair	*clear*	:soleil	*sun*	11
3.	musique	*music*	note	*note*	/disque	*disk*	11
4.	maladie	*illness*	lit	*bed*	/malade	*sick*	9
5.	homme	*man*	femme	*woman*	=femme		37
6.	profond	*deep*	puits	*well*	/plafond	*ceiling*	6
7.	mou	*soft*	dur	*hard*	/vache	*cow*	13
8.	manger	*eat*	boire	*drink*	=boire		28
9.	montagne	*mountain*	neige	*snow*	=neige		8
10.	maison	*house*	toit	*roof*	:jardin	*garden*	13
11.	noir	*black*	blanc	*white*	=blanc		53
12.	agneau	*lamb*	doux	*soft*	:mouton	*sheep*	7
13.	confort	*comfort*	fauteuil	*armchair*	/confortable	*comfortable*	5
14.	main	*hand*	pied	*foot*	=pied		19
15.	petit	*small*	grand	*large*	=grand		68

	STIMULUS		**NS RESPONSE**		**NNS RESPONSE**		**#**
16.	fruit	*fruit*	pomme	*apple*	=pomme		31
17.	papillon	*butterfly*	fleur	*flower*	=fleur		7
18.	lisse	*smooth*	rugueux	*rough*	/livre	*book*	10
19.	ordre	*order*	désordre	*disorder*	/demander	*ask*	7
20.	chaise	*chair*	table	*table*	=table		55
21.	doux	*soft*	dur	*hard*	/deux	*two*	14
22.	sifflet	*whistle*	train	*train*	/soufflé	*blow*	9
23.	femme	*woman*	homme	*man*	=homme		42
24.	froid	*cold*	chaud	*hot*	=chaud		56
25.	lent	*slow*	rapide	*rapid*	:vite	*fast*	10
26.	désirer	*desire*	vouloir	*want*	=vouloir		15
27.	rivière	*river*	fleuve	*large river*	:mer	*sea*	10
28.	blanc	*white*	noir	*black*	=noir		55
29.	beau (m.)	*beautiful*	joli	*pretty*	/belle (f.)	*beautiful*	15
30.	fenêtre	*window*	rideau	*screen, curtain*	:porte	*door*	31
31.	rugueux	*rough*	lisse	*smooth*	/rouge	*red*	16
32.	citoyen	*citizen*	vote	*vote*	/auto	*car*	12
33.	pied	*foot*	chaussure	*shoe*	:main	*hand*	20
34.	araignée	*spider*	toile	*web*	/arranger	*arrange*	5
35.	aiguille	*needle*	fil	*thread*	/train	*train*	2
36.	rouge	*red*	noir	*black*	:bleu	*blue*	14
37.	sommeil	*sleep*	lit	*bed*	/soleil	*sun*	15
38.	colère	*anger*	rouge	*red*	/bleu	*blue*	7
39.	tapis	*carpet*	moëlleux	*soft, velvety*	/eau	*water*	5
40.	fille	*girl*	garçon	*boy*	=garçon		28
41.	haut	*high*	bas	*low*	:montagne	*mountain*	4
42.	travail	*work*	repos	*rest*	/école	*school*	11
43.	aigre	*sour*	doux	*sweet*	/tigre	*tiger*	6
44.	terre	*land*	mer	*sea*	:ciel	*sky*	15
45.	difficulté	*difficulty*	facilité	*ease*	:facile	*easy*	18
46.	soldat	*soldier*	guerre	*war*	=guerre		6
47.	chou	*cabbage*	fleur	*flower*	/chat	*cat*	5
48.	dur	*hard*	mou	*soft*	/sur	*on*	4
49.	aigle	*eagle*	oiseau	*bird*	=oiseau		12
50.	estomac	*stomach*	digestion	*digestion*	:manger	*eat*	4
51.	tige	*stem*	fleur	*flower*	:tigre	*tigre*	16
52.	lampe	*lamp*	lumière	*light*	/lit	*bed*	9
53.	rêve	*dream*	sommeil	*sleep*	:dormir	*to sleep*	9
54.	jaune	*yellow*	vert	*green*	/vieux	*old*	14
55.	pain	*bread*	vin	*wine*	:beurre	*butter*	26
56.	justice	*justice*	balance	*balance*	/police	*police*	7
57.	garçon	*boy*	fille	*girl*	=fille		37
58.	clair	*clear*	obscur	*obscure*	:lune	*moon*	19
59.	santé	*health*	maladie	*illness*	/noël	*Christmas*	11
60.	évangile	*evangelist*	bible	*bible*	:église	*church*	11
61.	mémoire	*memory*	souvenir	*remember*	/tête	*head*	13
62.	mouton	*sheep*	doux	*soft*	/vache	*cow*	10
63.	bain	*bath*	mer	*sea*	:salle de bain	*bathroom*	13
64.	villa	*villa*	mer	*sea*	:maison	*house*	48
65.	rapide	*rapid*	train	*train*	:vite	*fast*	29
66.	bleu	*bleu*	mer	*sea*	:rouge	*red*	19
67.	faim	*hunger*	soif	*thirst*	:manger	*eat*	20
68.	prêtre	*priest*	noir	*black*	/prendre	*take*	18
69.	océan	*ocean*	mer	*sea*	=mer		23
70.	tête	*head*	cheveux	*hair*	:yeux	*eyes*	10
71.	fourneau	*oven*	cuisine	*kitchen*	/tourneau	*non-word*	3
72.	long	*long*	court	*short*	:petit	*small*	18
73.	religion	*religion*	église	*church*	=église		24

	STIMULUS		NS RESPONSE		NNS RESPONSE		#
74.	cognac	*cognac*	alcool	*alcohol*	:boire	*drink*	17
75.	enfant	*child*	petit	*small*	:bébé	*baby*	21
76.	amer	*bitter*	doux	*sweet*	/aimer	*love*	13
77.	marteau	*hammer*	pilon	*pestle*	/manteau	*coat*	3
78.	soif	*thirst*	faim	*hunger*	=faim		11
79.	ville	*city*	Paris		:maison	*house*	21
80.	carré	*square*	rond	*round*	/voiture	*car*	10
81.	beurre	*butter*	jaune	*yellow*	:pain	*bread*	44
82.	docteur	*doctor*	maladie	*illness*	:hôpital	*hospital*	19
83.	bruyant	*noisy*	enfant	*child*	/brille	*shine*	6
84.	voleur	*thief*	bicyclette	*bike*	:cambrioleur	*burglar*	5
85.	lion	*lion*	crinière	*mane*	:tigre	*tiger*	32
86.	joie	*joy*	tristesse	*sadness*	/joli	*pretty*	17
87.	lit	*bed*	repos	*rest*	:dormir	*sleep*	17
88.	lourd	*heavy*	léger	*light*	/silence	*silence*	4
89.	tabac	*tobacco*	fumée	*smoke*	:pipe	*pipe*	9
90.	bébé	*baby*	rose	*rose*	:enfant	*child*	33
91.	lune	*moon*	nuit	*night*	:clair	*clear*	13
92.	ciseaux	*scissors*	couper	*cut*	/cheveux	*hair*	7
93.	tranquille	*tranquil*	calme	*calm*	:silence	*silence*	6
94.	vert	*green*	pré	*meadow*	:bleu	*blue*	15
95.	sel	*salt*	mer	*sea*	/acheter	*buy*	6
96.	rue	*street*	maison	*house*	=maison		13
97.	roi	*king*	reine	*queen*	=reine		13
98.	fromage	*cheese*	blanc	*white*	:pain	*bread*	16
99.	fleur	*flower*	rose	*rose*	:jardin	*garden*	9
100.	effrayer	*frighten*	peur	*fear*	:enfant	*child*	4

QUESTIONS

1.   Divide the words within the nonnative speaker response column into the three association categories marked =, :, and /. Which is the largest category?

2.   Describe the differences in the kinds of words in the different columns: that is, decide why some words evoke native-like responses and others do not.

3.   Describe the associations in the category marked / (non-French associations). Do these associations rely mainly on *form* or on *meaning*?

4.   How would you interpret the responses provided by the learners to the stimuli *mou* (#7), *citoyen* (#32), *jaune* (#54), and *sel* (#95)?

Part Two

The following table reports the range of responses produced to the stimulus word *pain* (# 55) by native speakers of French (NSF) and by non-native speakers of French (NNSF)—native speakers of English. Words with only one response are not included.

			NSF	NNSF
1.	vin	*wine*	30	--
2.	blanc	*white*	19	--
3.	manger	*to eat*	19	4
4.	faim	*hunger*	16	--
5.	mie	*crumb*	14	--
6.	dur	*hard*	13	--
7.	nourriture	*food*	12	--
8.	sec	*dry*	11	--
9.	bis	*again (pain bis=whole meal)*	9	--
10.	quotidien	*daily*	8	--
11.	boulanger	*baker*	7	--
12.	beurre	*butter*	6	28
13.	blé	*corn*	5	--
14.	farine	*flour*	5	--
15.	amour	*love*	4	--
16.	bon	*good*	4	--
17.	frais	*fresh*	4	--
18.	noir	*black*	4	--
19.	aliment	*food*	3	--
20.	miche	*round loaf*	3	--
21.	sel	*salt*	3	--
22.	viande	*meat*	3	--
23.	boulangerie	*bakery*	2	--
24.	brûlé	*burnt*	2	--
25.	couteau	*knife*	2	3
26.	croissant	*croissant*	2	--
27.	croûte	*crust*	2	--
28.	cuisine	*kitchen*	2	--
29.	épice(s)	*spice(s)*	2	--
30.	lait	*milk*	2	2
31.	main	*hand*	2	--
32.	pauvre	*poor*	2	--
33.	repas	*meal*	2	--
34.	sucre	*sugar*	2	--
35.	table	*table*	2	--
36.	travail	*work*	2	--
37.	vie	*life*	2	--
38.	gâteau	*cake*	--	3
39.	fromage	*cheese*	--	2
40.	eau	*water*	--	2
41.	malade	*ill*	--	2
42.	doigt	*finger*	--	2

The following table reports the range of responses produced to the stimulus word *pain* (# 55) by native speakers of English. Words with only one response are not included.

1.	beurre	*butter*	28
2.	manger	*to eat*	4
3.	couteau	*knife*	3
4.	gâteau	*cake*	3
5.	fromage	*cheese*	2
6.	eau	*water*	2
7.	lait	*milk*	2
8.	malade	*ill*	2
9.	doigt	*finger*	2

QUESTIONS

5.   Describe the differences between the associations produced by native French speakers and those produced by learners and identify those that clearly rely on similarity between the L1 and the L2.

6.   What proportion of the learner associations can be described as native-like?

7.   What do these findings suggest about the organization of lexical knowledge in the learner's interlanguage?

SECTION THREE

Syntax and Semantics

1. do-fronting   stage 3

wh-
~~wh~~ inversion w/ wh   5

6. do fronting
      terse

Part One

Native Language:	Japanese
Target Language:	English
Data Source:	Spontaneous speech
Learner Information:	
Age:	5;4 (beginning of data collection) to 6;5 (end of data collection)
Gender:	Female
Age of First Exposure:	4;11
Learning Environment:	Play with children in U.S.
Number of Subjects:	1

LINGUISTIC BACKGROUND

Japanese word order is SOV (subject-object-verb). To form questions an interrogative particle *ka* is placed at the end of the sentence. There is no inversion of subject and verb and wh- words do not necessarily appear in sentence initial position, as can be seen below:

Are-wa nan desu-ka?
that what is   Q
"What is that?"

Month	Present Tense	Past Tense
1	Do you know? How do you do it? Do you have coffee? Do you want this one?	
2	What do you doing, this boy? What do you do it, this, froggie? What do you doing?	
3	Why do you do? How do you make? How do you draw that?	
4	What do you do?	Where did you get that?
5	How do you break it?	What did she say? What did you say? What did you say?
6	Do you bought too? Do you bought this too? Do you put it? Do you put it? How do you put it? How do you put it?	What did you do? What did you say?
7	How do you do it?	How did you get it?
8	Do you saw these peppermint? Do you saw some star eye? Do you saw some star eye?	Did you call? Did everybody saw some blue hairs?

9   Did you see the ghost?
                                           Did you know we locked the door
                                           when we come to here?

10   Did you use some blue?
                                           Why did you do that?

                                           Why did you get this?
                                           Why did you go to a hospital?
                                           Why did you draw?

11   What did you say?
                                           What did camel say?
                                           Did I make that?
                                           Did I make that?
                                           Did you see that?
                                           Did you see me?
                                           Why did you put this?
                                           I didn't correct this one, did I?

12   Did you what?

QUESTIONS

1.   Consider the way this child forms questions at Month 1. What kind of generalization has she made about English questions?

2.   Now consider the child's questions at Month 2. Is the child using the same generalization as she was at Month 1? What additional information do the data at Month 2 provide about the interpretation of the data at Month 1?

3.   Describe this child's use of wh- words.

4.   Describe all instances of past tense questions during Months 6-8.

5.   How would you describe the development of this child's knowledge of question formation? What evidence can you bring to bear to support your conclusions?

6.   What additional evidence would you like to see to support your analysis? (Be as specific as possible.)

========= **Part Two** =========

Native Language: Norwegian
Target Language: English
Data Source: Spontaneous speech and translation. (Data were collected four times at 3-4 week intervals. Translation tests were given 1 week after conversational data were collected.)

Learner Information:
    Age: 6;6 to 6;8
    Gender: Male
    Learning Environment: In school in Scotland
    Number of Subjects: 1

LINGUISTIC BACKGROUND

Norwegian has an auxiliary *ha* equivalent to the English *have*. There is no equivalent of English *do* in Norwegian questions. Questions are formed by inversion of subject and verb in the case of Yes/No questions as can be seen in the following:

Gjorde du det?
did   you it
'Did you do it?'

and by placing the wh- word at the beginning of the sentence in the case of wh- questions, as in the following example:

Hva sa han?
what said he
'What did he say?'

DATA

TIME 1
What you reading to-yesterday?
What she (is) doing now?
Can I give that to Sooty?

TIME 2
What d'you like? (When asked to repeat the sentence slowly, the child said:)
            What 'you like?
Eating you dinner to-yesterday?
Climb you?

TIME 3
What d'you do to-yesterday?
What d'you did to-yesterday?
When d'you went there?
What you did in Rothbury?
What you do in the hayshed?
Like you ice cream?
Did you drive car to-yesterday?
See you not on T.V. to-yesterday?
Say it you not to daddy?
Like you me not, Reidun?

TIME 4
Did you not see on T.V. to-yesterday?
Did you not say it to daddy?
Don't you like me Reidun?

QUESTIONS

7.   Describe this child's use of English questions at each point in time. Describe the differences you note among the four data collection periods and the progression of this child's knowledge of English questions.

*8.   Compare the description of this child's acquisition of questions with that of the child in Part One. To what extent does the native language seem to play a role in the acquisition of English questions?

*9.   What evidence do these data (Parts One and Two) suggest concerning discontinuity versus gradualness of acquisition?

PROBLEM 3.2

NEGATION

Native Language:	Spanish
Target Language:	English
Data Source:	Spontaneous speech
Background Information	Adult immigrant in the United States
Number of Subjects	1
Age	33
Gender	Male

Part One

Data

Week 1
Don't remember how you say it.
We don't know how automobile.
I don't understand.
I don't have time to go to college.

Week 3
I don't have the car.
I no understand.
No remember.
No understand that.
No have pronunciation.
No is mine.
Because no gain for the year.

Week 7
I no understand.
I no understand this question.
I no make, no can repeat the (oración),[1] no?
I don't can explain.

Week 11
I don't talk English.
I don't can more.
I don't understand this name.
I no like my coffee.
I no can explain this.
You no will come here this vacation:

Week 17
I don't understand.
I don't have a woman.
I no remember.

In my country no haves too much friends.
No like more, thank you.
No talk to him.

Week 21
I no like this summer.
Maybe no like this state.
I no have friend.
I no have application
No is problem.
I no can walk.

Week 27
No eat meat.
I don't saw.
People don't can pass the jungle.
No can make nothing.
No put sick.
Maybe she no live more.

Week 33
I don't understand this question.
I don't remember this name.
I no speak English very nice, no?
I no remember this name.
This isn't a supper, is a lunch.
No is good place.

Week 35
I don't care.
I don't understand.
No have sister.
I no eat nothing.
No drink nothing.
I don't can explain this picture.

QUESTIONS

1. Describe the subject's negative structures as they develop over time.

2. Describe his auxiliary structures (*do, is,* modal words) as they develop over time.

3. If you consider *don't* as a formulaic expression, what overall analysis can you provide for this learner's development of negation?

══

════════ **Part Two** ════════

Elicited Data[2] (change sentences to negatives)

JOHN, COME AT FIVE O'CLOCK.
    John, don't come in five o'clock.
SIT DOWN THERE.
    No sit.
COME AT FIVE O'CLOCK.
    I no come.
THE BOY WANTS A COOKIE.
    He no eat cookie.
SHE WANTS SOME DINNER.
    She don't want some dinner.
HE WENT OUTSIDE.
    He no, not come outside.
THE GIRL ATE SOME SOUP.
    He not eat soup.

SHE SAW HIM.
    She don't saw him.
THE GIRL ASKED SOMEONE.
    She don't answer.
THE BABY IS CRYING.
    She is don't crying.
SOMEBODY IS COMING IN.
    They don't come in.
THE DOG CAN BARK.
    The dog don't can bark.
THE GLASS WILL BREAK.
    Glass, it does, don't break.

QUESTIONS

4. Consider the elicited data above. In what ways are they similar to or different from the data gathered spontaneously (Part 1)?

---

[1] *Oración* translates as *sentence.*
[2] The first sentence listed in capital letters is the stimulus, the second sentence is the response.

PROBLEM 3.3

ADVERB PLACEMENT

Native Language:	French
Target Language:	English
Data Source:	Acceptability judgments; word manipulation task (learners were asked to form sentences); preference task
Learner Information:	
Age:	11-12 years
Learning Environment:	Intensive ESL program in Quebec
Proficiency Level:	Beginners (5 months of instruction)
Number of Subjects:	2 experimental groups
	a. adverb group = 82
	b. question group = 56
	Control group = 26

LINGUISTIC BACKGROUND

French and English differ with respect to adverb placement. In French, an adverb (A) may appear between the present tense verb (V) and its direct object (O) [SVAO], whereas in English it may not.

(1)   a.   Jean embrasse embrasse souvent Marie.
           b.   *John kisses often Mary.

French and English also differ with respect to question formation. In French, the main verb can invert with the (pronominal) subject to form a question, as in (3a). In contrast, English does not allow subject-verb inversion but rather requires subject-auxiliary inversion, as in (3c).

(2)   a.   Aime-t-elle Jean?
           b.   *Likes she John?
           c.   Does she like John?

METHODOLOGICAL BACKGROUND

All learners were pretested on adverb placement after approximately 3 months in an English language program. Up to this point, no classes had had any instruction on adverbs. Learners were divided into two groups: one group (Adverb group) received teaching materials and activities only on adverb placement for 2 weeks, whereas the other (Question group) was taught only question formation during the same period. All classes were then retested on adverb placement (first post-test). A second post-test was administered at the end of the intensive program (about five weeks after the first). The research design is summarized below:

36

Adverb Placement Study: Research Design

	Adv. Group. (n=82) Grades 5 and 6	Quest. Group (n=56) Grades 5 and 6	Control Group (n=26) Grades 4 and 5
Pretest (Day 1)	Pretesting adverbs	Pretesting adverbs	Testing on adverbs
Teaching (2 weeks)	Teaching adverbs	Teaching questions	
1st post-test (Day 15)	Post-test adverbs	Post-test adverbs	
2nd post-test (Day 50)	Post-test adverbs	Post-test adverbs	

The learners performed three tasks:
   (1) Acceptability Judgment Task

      Learners had to read a cartoon story and indicate instances of incorrect word orders. There were 33 sentences in the story broken down as follows:

         16 adverb positions (both grammatical and ungrammatical)
         10 grammatical distractors
         7 ungrammatical distractors

   (2) Preference Task

      Subjects read pairs of sentences and had to circle one of the responses beneath the sentences as below:

        a. Linda always takes the metro.
        b. Linda takes always the metro.

      only a is right   only b is right   both right   both wrong   don't know

      There were 32 sentence pairs, of which 4 were distractors.

   (3) Manipulation Task

      Subjects were tested individually. They were given a set of cards, each with one word on it (one card had an adverb). Subjects had to order the cards to make a grammatical English sentence. They were then asked if they could make yet another sentence. This was repeated until subjects could make no more sentences. Some card sets had intransitive verbs and prepositional phrases, others had transitive verbs and objects. Hence the labeling for these results are in the form SVAX (see Figure 3).

      Each subject performed this task with four sets of cards.

Part One

RESULTS

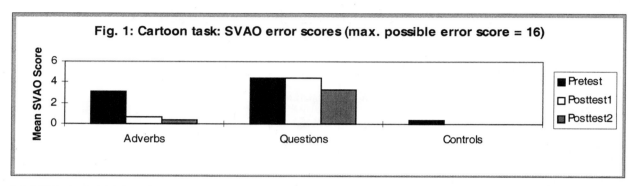
Fig. 1: Cartoon task: SVAO error scores (max. possible error score = 16)

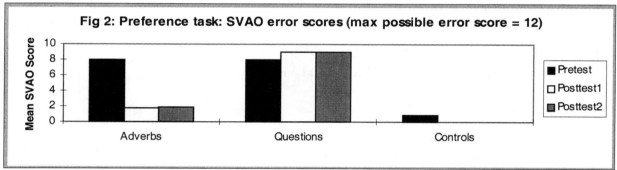
Fig 2: Preference task: SVAO error scores (max possible error score = 12)

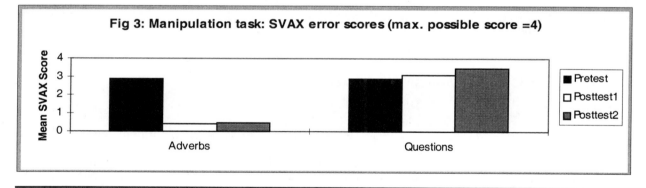
Fig 3: Manipulation task: SVAX error scores (max. possible score = 4)

QUESTIONS

1. Describe and explain the pattern of judgments of Francophone learners in the pretest.

2. Describe the patterns of responses given by the Adverb group and by the Question group in the first post-test. How would you account for the difference between them?

3. How would you characterize the differences between the pretest and the post-test in judgments on adverb placement?

4. What do these findings suggest about the role of instruction?

*5. On the basis of these findings, does instruction focused on one property (in this case questions) generalize to a different property (adverb placement)?

======== **Part Two** ========

A follow-up study was conducted 1 year after the original testing. Following are the results.

Fig. 4: Follow-up study, Judgment task: SVAO error scores

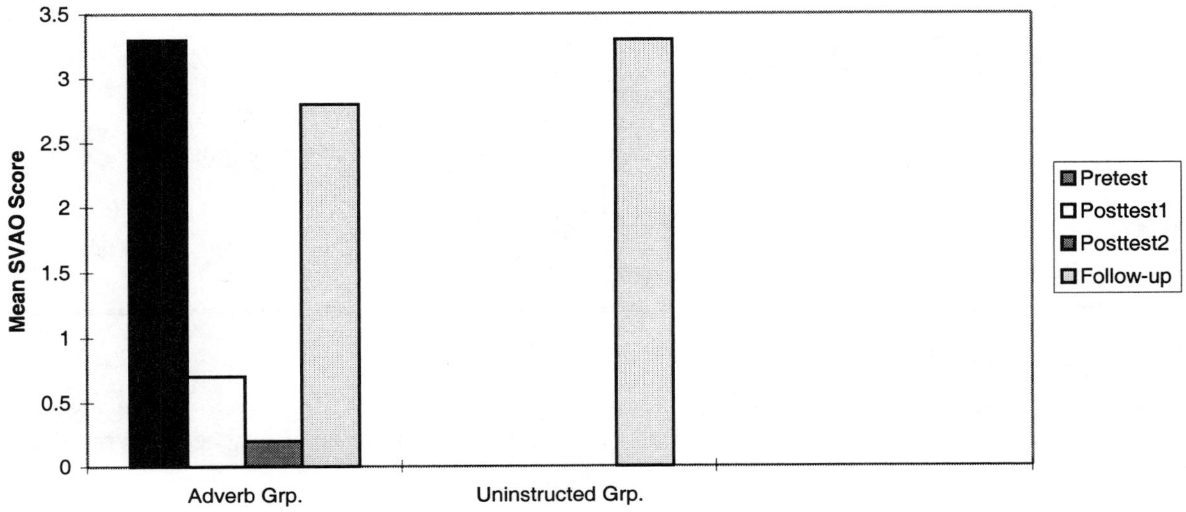

QUESTIONS

6.   Describe the results of the follow-up study. How do you interpret the fact that subjects revert to the pre-instruction SVAO score?

7.   Students continued their English language study between the second post-test and the follow-up. Why then is there noticeable regression?

8.   What generalization can you make about the effectiveness of instruction?

SUBJACENCY

Native Language:	Chinese, Korean, Indonesian
Target Language:	English
Data Source:	Acceptability judgments
Learner Information:	
Age:	Adults (average age = 21)
Age of First Exposure:	Indonesian = 13;1
	Chinese = 13;9
	Korean = 15;2
Proficiency Level:	Advanced (average: 6 years of exposure)
Number of Subjects:	20 Chinese
	21 Korean
	20 Indonesian
	19 English

THEORETICAL BACKGROUND

The principle of Subjacency constrains wh- movement, determining how far away a moved constituent can be from its original position. This accounts for the difference in acceptability between the sentences in (1):

(1)   a.   Henry said that Sue had bought a necklace.
            What did Henry say that Sue had bought?
      b.   Sam believed the claim that Carol had bought a necklace.
            *What did Sam believe the claim that Carol had bought?

In English, extraction of subjects and objects may take place from all of the following domains: adjuncts, relative clauses, noun phrase complements, embedded questions.

Indonesian allows wh- movement, but only of subjects. Chinese does not allow wh- extraction, but it does allow other types of extractions, therefore showing limited evidence of Subjacency. Korean does not allow any type of extraction and therefore shows no evidence of Subjacency at the level of S-structure. The differences among these languages can be summarized as follows:

	wh- Movement	Extraction (Subjacency)
English	Yes	Yes
Chinese	No	Yes
Indonesian	Yes (subjects only)	Yes
Korean	No	No

METHODOLOGICAL BACKGROUND

Learners were asked to judge sentences involving ungrammatical wh- extractions in four different constructions (Subjacency Test), as well as sentences involving the same constructions but in declarative form (Syntax Test). They were presented with the following eight sentence types and were asked to judge their acceptability:

Ungrammatical wh- extraction
     1.   *Which party did for Sam to join shock his parents? (sentential subject)
     2.   *Who did the police have evidence that the mayor murdered? (noun complement)
     3.   *Which problem did Bill find a principle which solves? (relative clause)
     4.   *Who did the police wonder who saw? (embedded question)

Grammatical constructions in declarative form
  5.   That oil prices will rise again this year is nearly certain. (sentential subject)
  6.   There is a good possibility that we can obtain the information elsewhere. (noun complement)
  7.   The professor that gave the most interesting lectures just left for Harvard. (relative clause)
  8.   The police didn't discover who the murderer was. (embedded question)

The design is given below:

SYNTAX

	PASS	FAIL
S U B J A C E N C Y	A	B
	C	D

Hypotheses:
  (1)   Learners who demonstrate a knowledge of a construction (i.e., pass the Syntax Test) will also show knowledge of Subjacency constraints (i.e., pass the Subjacency Test). They will fall into cell A.

  (2)   Learners who do not demonstrate knowledge of a construction (i.e., fail the Syntax Test) will also fail to demonstrate knowledge of Subjacency constraints (i.e., fail the Subjacency Test). They will fall into cell D.

=======   **Part One**   =======

RESULTS

The results below are based on an average of the subjects' performance in all sentence types.

SYNTAX

	English n=19		Indonesian n=20		Chinese n=20		Korean n=21	
	PASS	FAIL	PASS	FAIL	PASS	FAIL	PASS	FAIL
	14	1.7	7	.7	8.7	1.7	3.2	.5
	2.7	.5	9	3	7.7	1.7	10.7	6.5
	= 18.9		= 19.7		=19.8		= 20.9	

QUESTIONS

1.   Describe the distribution of responses for native and nonnative speakers reported above. How do the learners judge Subjacency violations in English?

2.   Which hypothesis is confirmed by the pattern of native speaker responses?

3.   Which hypothesis is confirmed by the pattern of nonnative speaker responses?

4.   Identify differences in the nonnative responses due to language background. How can these differences be interpreted?

5.   What conclusion do these findings suggest about the acquisition of Subjacency constraints in English L2?

6.   Show how the native language facts relate to the L2 findings.

===============   **Part Two**   ===============

In the table below are the results based on three (sentential subjects are not included) of the four sentence types representing Subjacency violations. The numbers represent subjects' performance on the Syntax and Subjacency tests (see methodological background).

Language	Relative Clauses		Noun Complements		Embedded Questions	
English	17	1	10	1	14	2
	0	1	7	1	3	0
Indonesian	6	1	8	0	8	1
	9	4	11	1	6	5
Chinese	10	0	11	0	7	2
	6	4	9	0	9	2
Korean	5	0	2	0	3	0
	8	8	15	4	13	5

QUESTIONS

7.   Describe the distribution of responses for native and nonnative speakers on the basis of sentence types.

8.   What differences do you note among the sentence types? What differences do you notice among the language groups?

9.   Account for the differences you noted.

*10.   Having considered these data, speculate on the availability of Universal Grammar in second language acquisition.

PROBLEM 3.5

Near-nativeness 1

Native Language: English, Italian, Chinese, Farsi, Spanish, German, Japanese, Korean, Portuguese

Target Language: French

Data Source: Acceptability judgments

Learner Information:

    Age: Adults

    Length of Residence: 5.5 - 30 years (average = 17.4 years)

    Learning Environment: Foreign language classroom and naturalistic exposure in France

    Proficiency Level: Near-native

    Number of Subjects: Near-native speakers = 21
Native speakers = 20

LINGUISTIC BACKGROUND

Two groups of subjects (21 near-native speakers of French and 20 native speakers of French) were tested on the following French constructions.

- **_Il/elle_ versus _ce_** (he/she versus this)

  Example:
  > Qui est Victor Hugo (Who is Victor Hugo?)
  > *Il est un grand écrivain. (He is a great writer.)
  > C'est un grand écrivain. (This is a great writer.)

- **Place of adjectives**

  Example:
  > J'ai une douce amie à Paris. (I have a girlfriend in Paris.)
  > J'ai une amie douce à Paris. (I have a gentle friend in Paris.)

- **_Imparfait_ and _passé composé_** (imperfect and present perfect)

  Example:
  > Est-ce que tu as su conduire dans la neige? (Did you manage to drive in the snow?)
  > Est-ce que tu savais conduire dans la neige. (Did you know how to drive in the snow?)

- **_à/de_ + infinitive**

  Example:
  > Il se fatigue à/de voir les enfants jouer. (He is getting tired of seeing the children play.)

- **_de_ + adjective**

  Example:
  > Encore un problème de résolu. (One more problem resolved.)

- **Object + predicate**

  Example:
  > *Paul assure Virginie heureuse. (Paul assures Virginie [to be] happy)
  > On l'assure heureuse. (People assure her [to be] happy)

- **Articles**

  Example:
  > C'était le soir; des/les gens se promenaient à la nuit tombante. (It was evening; people were walking at nightfall.)
  > Ici, en France,*des/les gens ne savent souvent plus conduire en hiver. (Here, in France, people often don't know how to drive any more in winter.)

══════   **Part One**   ══════

An average score for the native speakers was calculated, called an evaluation index. This constituted the native speaker norm—(10%).

The figures below represent the divergent scores (% of divergence) of both native speakers (Figure 1), and near-native speakers (Figure 2). Each bar represents an individual speaker.

Fig. 1: Percentage of Divergence of Native Speakers

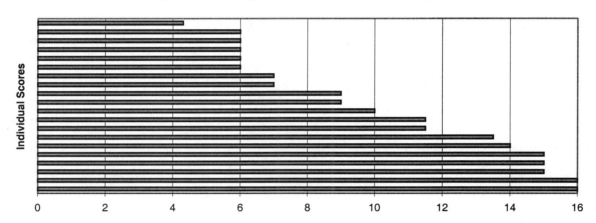

Fig. 2: Percentage of Divergence of Near-Native Speakers

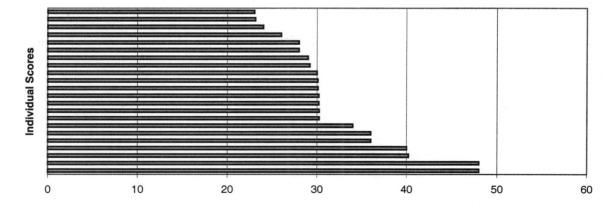

QUESTIONS

1.   Consider the native speaker results in Figure 1. What is the range of the percentage of divergence from the native speaker norm? Consider the near-native speaker results in Figure 2. What is the range of the percentage of divergence from the native speaker norm?

2.   Describe the difference between the native speaker and near-native speaker percentages of divergence.

==========   **Part Two**   ==========

RESULTS

The following table gives an analysis of the deviation from the native speaker norm according to grammatical structure.

Grammatical Structure [# of tokens in ( )]	Native	Near-native
Il/elle vs. *ce* (10)	10.0%	35.7%
Place of the Adj. (14)	11.8%	38.1%
Imperf. vs. Pres. Perf. (5)	2.0%	41.5%
á/de + Infinitive (2)	6.0%	40.7%
de + Adj. (10)	6.0%	22.9%
Obj. + Pred. (28)	14.3%	33.2%
Articles (8)	15.0%	34.9%

QUESTIONS

3.   Compare the orderings of the native and near-native speakers. To what extent are they similar or different?

4.   How would you interpret the differences between the native and the near-native groups?

========   **Part Three**   ========

RESULTS

Below is the percentage of divergence from the norm by native language group. Numbers in ( ) are the number of speakers in that group.

Grammatical Structure	Romance (7)	Germanic (7)	Farsi (2)	Japanese/Korean/ Chinese(5)
Il/elle vs. *ce*	35.7%	30.0%	55.0%	36.0%
Place of the Adj.	32.3%	37.1%	46.4%	44.1%
Imperf. vs. Pres. Perf.	19.2%	38.2%	50.0%	66.7%
á/de + infinitive	33.3%	44.4%	33.3%	50.0%
de + Adj.	27.1%	15.7%	26.0%	30.0%
Obj. + Pred.	36.7%	25.5%	37.5%	38.4%
Articles	41.7%	14.3%	62.5%	45.9%

QUESTIONS

5.   Consider the data that give the amount of divergence according to language background. In what way do the four language groups differ from one another? For each construction, compare the results across languages. For which are there differences? How do you account for the similarities and differences?

6.   If you know any of these source languages, can you be specific as to the source of the divergence from native speaker norms?

7.   Given that these speakers could pass as native at the level of production, how would you interpret the discrepancy between their acceptability judgments and their production?

8.   In this problem, we use the concept "near-native" and define it as "virtually indistinguishable from native speakers." In your opinion, what is it that makes a nonnative speaker near-native?

*9.   What implications are there for the Critical Period Hypothesis?

PROBLEM 3.6

NEAR-NATIVENESS 2

Native Language:	French, English
Target Language:	Italian
Data Source:	Acceptability judgments
Learner Information:	
Age:	Adults
Age of First Exposure:	18 - 27
Learning Environment:	Foreign language classroom and naturalistic exposure in Italy
Proficiency Level:	Near-native
Number of Subjects:	24 native speakers of English
	20 native speakers of French

Part One

LINGUISTIC BACKGROUND

Italian has two auxiliaries *avere* "to have" and *essere* "to be." For most verbs either one or the other auxiliary is used. However, there are some constructions that make the choice of auxiliary optional; there are others that make a change of auxiliary obligatory. The following constructions are possible in Italian:

Optional auxiliary change

    Mario ha dovuto andare a casa.   Mario è dovuto andare a casa.
    Mario has had to go to home   *Mario is had to go   to home*

                        'Mario had to go home.'

Obligatory auxiliary change   (with clitic [e.g., *ci*] movement)
    Mario ci   *ha dovuto andare.   Mario ci   è dovuto andare.
    Mario there has had   to go   *Mario there is had   to go*

                        'Mario had to go there.'

Optional auxiliary change (with no clitic [e.g., *ci*] movement)
    Mario ha dovuto andarci   Mario è dovuto andarci.
    Mario has had to go there   *Mario is had to go there*

                        'Mario had to go there.'

French has clitics and two auxiliaries (*avoir* "to have" and *être* "to be") but does not allow any of the phenomena described above for Italian.

English does not have either auxiliary choice or clitics.

METHODOLOGICAL BACKGROUND

Acceptability judgments were elicited by means of a *magnitude estimation* procedure (See Glossary).

RESULTS

Mean acceptability judgments on three Italian constructions (the higher the number, the more acceptable the sentence).

		INS	FNNS	ENNS
Optional AUX (basic)	*essere*	9.260	3.824	7.231
	avere	9.749	9.420	6.977
Clitic movement	*essere*	8.587	8.525	6.286
	avere	3.143	4.285	6.623
No movement	*essere*	8.159	4.065	6.784
	avere	8.779	7.841	6.211

INS = Italian native speakers; FNNS = French near-native speakers of Italian, ENNS = English near-native speakers of Italian

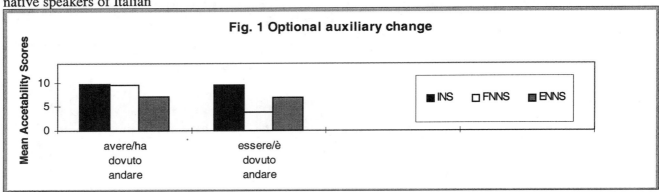

Fig. 1 Optional auxiliary change

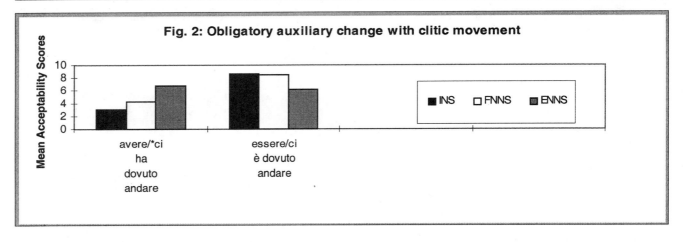

Fig. 2: Obligatory auxiliary change with clitic movement

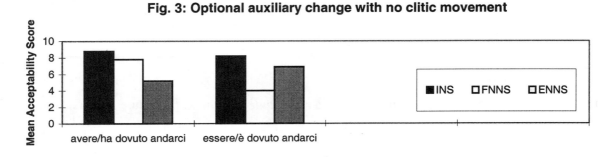

Fig. 3: Optional auxiliary change with no clitic movement

QUESTIONS

1. Describe the differences between the responses of the French near-native speakers and the English near-native speakers.

2. Consider the description of the facts of the three languages in question provided in the linguistic background. To what extent can the judgments of the two near-native groups be accounted for in terms of transfer from the L1?

3. These speakers had been exposed to these structures in the Italian input for many years. What do these data tell us about the role of exposure in second language acquisition?

*4. These speakers could pass as native at the level of production. How would you interpret the discrepancy between their acceptability judgments and their production? Consider that some of the rules are optional.

========   **Part Two**   ========

METHODOLOGICAL BACKGROUND

The same near-native speakers were also administered a card-sorting test, in which they had to arrange a series of cards (with the same sentences as in Part One, each printed individually on a separate card) in a sequence of piles according to their degree of acceptability. No limit was imposed as to the number of piles possible. Unlike the acceptability judgment test in Part One (which was a magnitude estimation procedure), the card-sorting test was self-paced and untimed.

RESULTS

Card-sorting task results are given below; higher numbers mean greater acceptability.

Mean acceptability judgments on three Italian constructions

		INS	FNNS	ENNS
Optional AUX	*essere*	4.944	4.000	4.042
(basic)	*avere*	5.167	4.650	5.042
Clitic movement	*essere*	4.667	4.050	4.125
	avere	3.750	3.300	3.792
No movement	*essere*	4.306	4.250	4.083
	avere	4.389	4.100	3.625

INS = Italian native speakers; FNNS = French near-native speakers of Italian, ENNS = English near-native speakers of Italian

Fig. 4: Optional auxiliary change

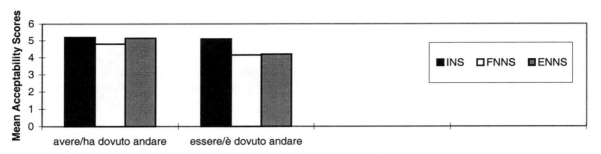

Fig. 5: Obligatory auxiliary change with clitic movement

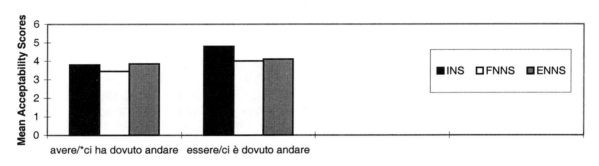

Fig. 6: Optional auxiliary change with no clitic movement

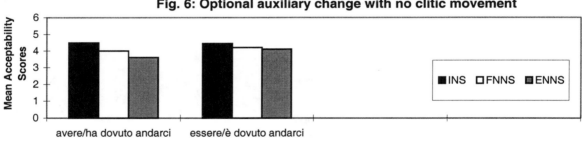

QUESTIONS

5.   Describe and interpret the responses given by French and English near-native speakers.

6.   Consider the conditions surrounding the two tasks in Parts One and Two. What differences are there in the tasks themselves that might account for the differences in responses?

*7. What conclusions can you draw about the type of knowledge attained at the near-native level and what are the implications for the Critical Period Hypothesis?

═══ PROBLEM 3.7 ═══

AUXILIARIES

Native Language:	English, French
Target Language:	Italian
Data Source:	Acceptability judgments (using magnitude estimation—see glossary)
Learner Information:	
Age:	Adults
Age of First Exposure:	18 - 27
Length of Exposure:	Range 5 to 15 years
Learning Environment:	Foreign language classroom and naturalistic exposure in Italy
Proficiency Level:	English speakers (beginning, intermediate, advanced, near-native); French (near-native)
Number of subjects:	24 English native speakers (near-native)
	20 French native speakers (near-native)
	32 beginners (native English speakers)
	36 intermediate (native English speakers)
	32 advanced (native English speakers)

═══ **Part One** ═══

LINGUISTIC BACKGROUND

Italian has two auxiliaries in compound tenses, *essere* "to be" and *avere* "to have." The choice of auxiliary depends on the type of verb. The present tense conjugations of these auxiliaries are as follows:

	avere	**essere**
1st sg.	ho	sono
2nd sg.	hai	sei
3rd sg.	ha	è
1st pl.	abbiamo	siamo
2nd pl.	avete	siete
3rd pl.	hanno	sono

DATA
1. Teresa ha scritto una lettera al suo fidanzato. (Teresa wrote a letter to her fiance.)
2. Le tasse sono aumentate del 20%. (Taxes have increased by 20%.)
3. Claudia ha studiato filosofia. (Claudia studied philosophy.)
4. Francesca è arrivata in ritardo all'appuntamento. (Francesca arrived late for her appointment.)
5. I dinosauri sono esistiti milioni di anni fa. (Dinosaurs existed millions of years ago.)
6. Paolo ha mangiato gli spaghetti. (Paolo ate the spaghetti.)
7. I bambini sono saltati giù dal letto. (The children jumped down from the bed.)
8. Paola è corsa in farmacia. (Paola ran to the drugstore.)
9. Carlo ha guardato la televisione. (Carlo watched television.)
10. Carla ha lavorato in ristorante l'anno scorso. (Carla worked in a restaurant last year.)
11. I bambini hanno ascoltato la musica. (The children played the music.)
12. Paola ha corso piú velocemente di tutti (Paula ran raster than everyone.)
13. Il governo ha aumentato i prezzi (The government has increased prices.)
14. Questa pipa è appartenuta a mio padre. (This pipe belonged to my father.)
15. Sara Simeoni ha saltato alla Olimpiadi di Mosca. (Sara S. jumped in the Moscow Olympics.)
16. Maria è venuta alla festa con il suo amico. (Maria came to the party with her boyfriend.)

17. Marco ha bagnato le piante. (Marco watered the plant.)
18. Dopo cena gli ospiti hanno giocato a carte. (After dinner the guests played cards.)
19. Franca ha dormito tutto il pomeriggio. (Franca slept the whole afternoon.)
20. Mio padre ha comprato il giornale. (My father bought the newspaper.)
21. Carla è restata da me fino a tardi. (Carla stayed at my house until late.)
22. Mia zia ha viaggiato molto da giovane. (My aunt travelled a lot when she was young.)
23. I miei nonni sono sopravvissuti al terremoto del 1908. (My grandparents survived the 1908 earthquake.)
24. La nave è affondata rapidamente. (The boat sank rapidly.)

QUESTIONS

1.   Divide the verbs in the sentences above into the categories transitive and intransitive. Which auxiliaries are used with transitive verbs? Which are used with intransitive verbs?

2.   The category of intransitive verbs can be further subdivided into verbs that select *avere* and verbs that select *essere* depending on the meaning of the verb. Divide those verbs you determined in Question 1 to be intransitive according to the following:
     a) 6 verbs denoting an activity with no change of state/location
     b) 2 verbs denoting the existence of a state
     c) 2 verbs denoting a change of state that can also be used transitively
     d) 4 verbs denoting a change of location
     e) 2 verbs denoting the continuation of a pre-existing state

3.   The intransitive verbs in (a) can be referred to as *unergative*; the ones in categories (b) through (e) can be referred to as *unaccusative*. Which auxiliary(ies) is/are used with unergative verbs and which with unaccusative verbs?

4.   Notice the pairs of sentences 8 & 12 and 7 & 15. The same verbs appear with different auxiliaries. What meaning components are associated with each auxiliary?

RESULTS

Figure. 1: Unaccusative verbs with *avere*

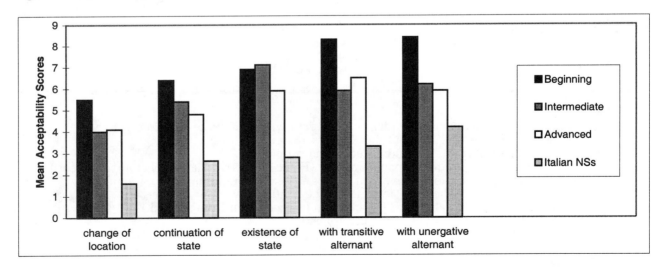

QUESTIONS

5.   From Figure 1, consider the pattern of native Italian judgments on *avere* with unaccusative verbs. Which verb type is the least acceptable with *avere*? Which verb type is the most acceptable with *avere*?

6.   For each proficiency level, order the verb types shown in Figure 1 from least to most acceptable with *avere*. What is the effect of proficiency level on the learners' ordering of verb types?

7.   Describe the development of these learners' knowledge of auxiliary selection.

8.   How would you interpret the scale of acceptability shown by Figure 1?

=========   **Part Two**   =========

LINGUISTIC BACKGROUND
French, like Italian has two auxiliaries in compound tenses: *être* "to be" and *avoir* "to have". However, *être* is used only with a small set of verbs, including the following: *aller* "to go," *tomber* "to fall," *arriver* "to arrive," *venir* "to come," *rester* "to rest," *devenir* and "to become." All other verbs use *avoir*.

RESULTS

Mean acceptability judgments on five categories of unaccusative verbs (*essere* and *avere* versions). The higher the number, the more acceptable the sentence.

		INS	FNNS	ENNS
Change of location	*essere*	9.509	9.927	9.248
	avere	1.653	1.875	2.224
Continuation of state	*essere*	9.704	9.160	8.228
	avere	2.665	3.417	3.214
Existence of state	*essere*	9.203	8.930	8.088
	avere	2.922	4.375	3.930
Verbs with a transitive alternant	*essere*	9.340	9.825	9.170
	avere	3.562	6.629	5.353
Verbs with unergative alternant	*essere*	9.686·	9.874	8.367
	avere	4.204	7.045	5.448

INS = Italian native speakers; FNNS = French native speakers (learners of Italian); ENNS = English native speakers (learners of Italian).

QUESTIONS

9.   Describe the judgments given by French near-native speakers on unaccusative verbs with *avere*.

10.   What differences are there between the judgments of French near-natives and those of English near-natives?

11.   Compare the two near-native groups with the native speakers of Italian. To what extent are there differences/similarities?

12.   Compare these data with the data presented in Problem 3.6. How would you account for the fact that there is little influence of the L1 in the data presented?

=========   **Part Three**   =========

DATA

Learners of English from non-Romance language backgrounds, such as Arabic, Japanese, and Thai have been found to produce sentences such as the following (written data).

1.   The most memorable experience of my life was happened 15 years ago. (L1 Arabic - advanced)
2.   Most of the people are fallen in love and marry with somebody. (Japanese L1 - high intermediate)
3.   My mother was died when I was a baby. (Thai L1 - high intermediate)

QUESTIONS

13.   Describe the nonstandard features in the sentences above.

14.   What type of verbs appear in these sentences?

15.   How would you interpret the use of auxiliaries in these sentences in the light of the conclusions you drew in Parts One and Two?

REFLEXIVES

Native Language:	Chinese, English
Target Language:	English, Chinese
Data Source:	Acceptability judgments (using magnitude estimation); interpretation task
Learner Information:	
Age:	Adults
Age of First Exposure:	After age 15
Learning Environment:	Foreign language classroom
Proficiency Level:	7 groups of nonnative speakers of English ranging from elementary to advanced
	5 groups of nonnative speakers of Chinese ranging from elementary to advanced
Number of Subjects:	159 learners of English
	102 learners of Chinese
	16 native speakers of English
	24 native speakers of Chinese

LINGUISTIC BACKGROUND

English and Chinese differ with respect to the interpretation of reflexives. Consider the following sentences:

(1)   a.   Wang Ping, renwei Zhang Bo, xiangxin ziji
                Wang Ping thinks Zhang Bo trust self

       b.   John thinks Bill trusts himself.

In (1a), the reflexive *ziji* can be interpreted as coreferential with either the subject in the main clause (Wang Ping) or the subject in the embedded clause (Zhang Bo). In contrast, in (1b) the reflexive *himself* in the equivalent English sentence can only be coreferential with the subject in the embedded clause (Bill).

In sum, in English, reflexives can only have an antecedent that is in the same clause (i.e., a local antecedent), whereas in Chinese, reflexives can have an antecedent that is outside of the clause (i.e., a long-distance antecedent).

A further difference between the two languages is the fact that in Chinese the reflexive can also appear in preverbal position, as in (2). English disallows this possibility.

(2)   a.   tade nüer cai san sui, danshi ziji yijing hui chuan yifu le
               his daughter only three age, but self already can put on clothes PART

       b.   *His daughter is only three but herself can put on her clothes.

PART = particle

METHODOLOGICAL BACKGROUND

Sentences were presented simultaneously in written and oral form. For those sentences with preverbal reflexives, acceptability judgments were elicited. A time limit of 9 seconds per sentence was imposed. For all other sentences, subjects were asked to judge which antecedent(s) are acceptable, as in (3) and (4) below.

(3) Peter thinks John doesn't have confidence in himself.
                himself =   a) Peter
                            b) John

(4) John thinks Bill trusts himself.
                himself =   a) John
                            b) Bill
A time limit of 12 seconds was imposed.

===================   **Part One**   ===================

RESULTS:

Chinese learners of English

Figure 1: Mean scores of judgments on three sentence types: 1) PR = preverbal reflexives; 2) local; 3) LDR = long-distance reflexives by the 7 EFL groups and native speakers of English. (The higher the number, the more acceptable the sentence.)

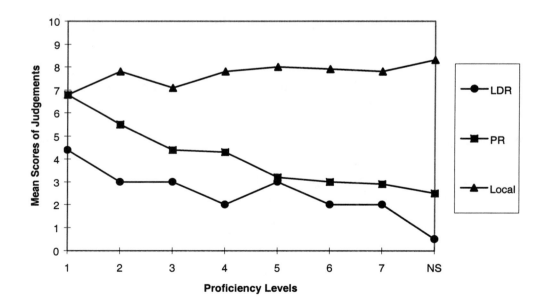

English learners of Chinese

Figure 2: Mean scores of judgments on three sentence types: 1) PR = preverbal reflexives; 2) local; 3) LDR = long-distance reflexives by the 5 CFL groups and native speakers of Chinese.

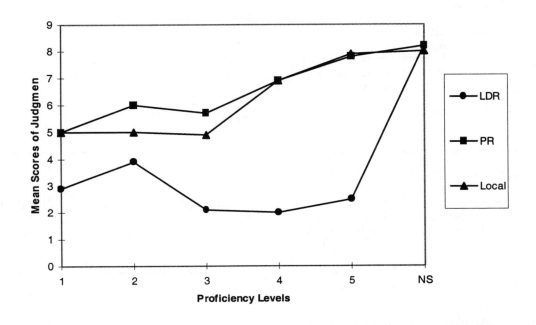

QUESTIONS

1. Describe the developmental trend of the judgments given by Chinese learners of English (EFL) at different proficiency levels (Figure 1). Identify contrasts that can be attributed to types of construction.

2. Describe the developmental trend of the judgments given by English learners of Chinese (CFL) at different proficiency levels (Figure 2). Identify contrasts that can be attributed to types of construction.

3. How would you interpret the asymmetry revealed by these data?

PROBLEM 3.9

VERBAL COMPLEMENTS

Native Language: Various
Target Language: English
Data Source: Sentence interpretation
Learner Information:
          Age: Adults
          Learning Environment: Intensive ESL Program, U.S.
          Proficiency Level: From Level 2 to Level 5 of a 5-level program
          Number of Subjects: Level 2 = 15
                                       Level 3 = 21
                                       Level 4 = 36
                                       Level 5 = 39

METHODOLOGICAL BACKGROUND

Learners were given the following sentences and were asked to determine the subject of the second clause. The sentences fall into two syntactic types, those that behave like sentences with *tell* and those that behave like sentences with *promise*. These sentences have the same syntactic structure but differ in their interpretation. (Consider *John promised Joan to come* vs. *John told Joan to come*.)

1.	The chair told the dog to leave.	*Who should leave?*
2.	The chair promised the dog to leave.	
3.	The chair told the table to leave.	
4.	The boy told the dog to leave.	
5.	The table promised the boy to leave.	
6.	The girl told the chair to leave.	
7.	The dog told the boy to leave.	
8.	The dog told the chair to leave.	
9.	The dog promised the cat to leave.	
10.	The table told the boy to leave.	
11.	The girl promised the chair to leave.	
12.	The dog promised the boy to leave.	
13.	The boy promised the girl to leave.	
14.	The boy promised the dog to leave.	
15.	The chair promised the table to leave.	
16.	The dog told the cat to leave.	
17.	The boy told the girl to leave.	
18.	The dog promised the chair to leave.	

=========   **Part One**   =========

QUESTIONS

1. For the 18 sentences listed in the Methodological Background section, identify which sentences belong to each of the two sentence types, *tell*-type and *promise*-type.

2. What are the main differences between the two sentence types? Who does the "going?"

=========   **Part Two**   =========

Consider the results for the *tell* and *promise* type sentences. In these tables, a response pattern such as 2-3 for a Human/Human sentence such as "The woman told the man to go home" means that two individuals responded that the woman was the subject of the second verb and three individuals responded that it was the man. Because not all sentences were given to all learners and because not all individuals responded to all sentences, the numbers in the results do not always add up to the number of individuals who participated in the study. In these tables, convergence means that the second noun (the subject of the lower clause) is higher on the animacy hierarchy (human>animate>inanimate) than the first noun. Divergence in these tables means that the first noun is higher on the animacy hierarchy than the second noun. For *promise* sentences, the opposite holds.

Table 1: Results of *tell* sentences in which both NPs are of equal status in semantic terms

Noun Phrases	Level 2	Level 3	Level 4	Level 5
Human/Human	2-3	1-9	0-10	1-14
Animate/Animate	1-4	1-8	1-11	1-13
Inanimate/Inanimate	2-3	0-9	6-8	1-15

Table 2: Results of *tell* sentences in which syntactic and semantic information converge

Noun Phrases	Level 2	Level 3	Level 4	Level 5
Inanimate/Animate	1-5	0-10	2-12	1-15
Inanimate/Human	1-8	3-8	1-7	0-8
Animate/Human	1-4	2-7	1-13	1-15

Table 3: Results of *tell* sentences in which syntactic and semantic information diverge

Noun Phrases	Level 2	Level 3	Level 4	Level 5
Animate/Inanimate	5-4	8-3	4-5	4-4
Human/Inanimate	3-2	5-4	6-8	1-15
Human/Animate	1-5	0-10	2-12	1-15

Table 4: Results of *promise* sentences in which both NPs are of equal status in semantic terms

Noun Phrases	Level 2	Level 3	Level 4	Level 5
Human/Human	8-1	7-4	8-1	8-0
Animate/Animate	6-3	8-3	6-3	8-0
Inanimate/Inanimate	7-2	8-1	9-3	13-0

Table 5: Results of *promise* sentences in which syntactic and semantic information converge

Noun Phrases	Level 2	Level 3	Level 4	Level 5
Animate/Inanimate	3-2	5-4	9-3	12-1
Human/Inanimate	7-2	9-2	8-1	8-0
Human/Animate	5-4	6-5	9-3	13-0

Table 6: Results of *promise* sentences in which syntactic and semantic information diverge

Noun Phrases	Level 2	Level 3	Level 4	Level 5
Inanimate/Animate	3-3	4-5	11-3	15-1
Inanimate/Human	2-4	5-5	9-5	14-2
Animate/Human	6-3	8-3	9-0	7-1

QUESTIONS

3. Classify the sentences into the categories given in the tables (e.g., for the *tell* sentences, human/human, animate/animate, inanimate/inanimate, inanimate/animate, inanimate/human, animate/human, etc.).

4. For the *tell* sentences, what differences are there among those sentences of equal status (Table 1), those sentences in which there is convergence (Table 2), and those sentences in which there is divergence (Table 3)? How does proficiency level affect the results?

5. To what extent are the results for the *promise* sentences consistent with those for the *tell* sentences?

6. Suggest an interpretation of these data. For example, what do they suggest about the relative importance of syntactic and semantic factors in second language acquisition?

PROBLEM 3.10

TENSE/ASPECT

Native Language:	Spanish (Part One), Japanese (Part Two)
Data Source:	Acceptability judgments
Learner Information:	
Age:	Adults
Learning Environment:	Students in an ESL program, U.S.
Proficiency Level:	Ranging from low intermediate to advanced
Number of Subjects:	52

THEORETICAL BACKGROUND

This problem deals with the various meanings of the progressive (-*ing*), the simple present and the future. Basic meanings are as follows: (1) progressive is: ongoing, witnessed activity that persists for an extended period of time; (2) simple present is: lawlike regular state or expected events characteristic of their subject at the present time; (3) future is: states or events expected in foreseeable future.

Part One

English Sentences	Spanish Speakers % total sentences judged "correct"
1. Dan sees better.	65
2. Dan is seeing better now.	81
3. Mary is being in Chicago now.	8
4. John is travelling to New York tomorrow.	8
5. The new bridge connects Detroit and Windsor.	79
6. The new bridge is connecting Detroit and Windsor.	46
7. John travels to New York tomorrow.	8
8. John will travel to New York tomorrow.	86
9. John is smoking American cigarettes now.	88
10. The new bridge will connect Detroit and Windsor.	67
11. Fred smokes American cigarettes now.	56
12. Mary will be in Chicago now.	10
13. John will smoke American cigarettes now.	10
14. Mary is in Chicago now.	88

QUESTIONS

1. Focus on the three verb tense/aspect forms: (1) progressive, (2) simple present, (3) future. For each, order the sentences from those with the greatest percentage of "correct" judgments to those with the lowest percentage of "correct" judgments. What explanation can you give for the differential acceptability of the various uses of each of the tense/aspects?

2. What do these data suggest about the interaction between syntax and semantics in second language acquisition?

3. Consider Sentence 7, the translation equivalent of which is possible in Spanish. The acceptability of this sentence is low. How can you account for this?

4. What does this suggest about the interaction between the native language and language universals?

=========   **Part Two**   =========

English Sentences	Japanese Speakers % total sentences judged "correct"
1. Dan sees better.	45
2. Dan is seeing better now.	19
3. Mary is being in Chicago now.	5
4. John is travelling to New York tomorrow.	32
5. The new bridge connects Detroit and Windsor.	73
6. The new bridge is connecting Detroit and Windsor.	24
7. John travels to New York tomorrow.	19
8. John will travel to New York tomorrow.	81
9. John is smoking American cigarettes now.	76
10. The new bridge will connect Detroit and Windsor.	87
11. Fred smokes American cigarettes now.	51
12. Mary will be in Chicago now.	14
13. John will smoke American cigarettes now.	3
14. Mary is in Chicago now.	92

QUESTIONS

5.   Focus on the three verb tense/aspect forms: (1) progressive, (2) simple present, (3) future. For each, order the sentences from those with the greatest percentage of "correct" judgments to those with the lowest percentage of "correct" judgments. What explanation can you give for the differential acceptability of the various uses of each of the tense/aspects?

6.   Is this order the same as the order established for the Spanish speakers? If not, where do you find differences? How do you account for the differences?

7.   Focus on those sentences where there appears to be similarity in responses between the Spanish and the Japanese speakers. Given that Spanish and Japanese are typologically distinct, how do you account for the similarities?

8.   What general comments can you make about the acquisition of tense/aspect systems?

SECTION FOUR

Phonology

PROBLEM 4.1

VOWEL EPENTHESIS

Native Language:	Egyptian Arabic and Iraqi Arabic
Target Language:	English
Data Source:	Recorded errors from a variety of sources
Learner Information:	
Age:	Adults

Part One

Below are examples of interlanguage forms produced by speakers of two varieties of Arabic:

Egyptian

[filoor]	floor
[bilastik]	plastic
[θirii]	three
[tiransilet]	translate
[silayd]	slide
[firɛd]	Fred
[tʃildiren]	children

Iraqi

[ifloor]	floor
[ibleen]	plane
[isnoo]	snow
[iθrii]	three
[istadi]	study
[ifrɛd]	Fred
[tʃilidren]	children

QUESTIONS

1. Many Arabic speakers tend to insert a vowel in their pronunciation of English words. Based on these data, what vowel do they insert and where?

2. State the rule that describes the interlanguage generalization that these learners have come up with.

===== **Part Two** =====

These varieties of Arabic have rules inserting vowels in certain positions in native language words. The application of these rules is illustrated below:

Egyptian Arabic

katabu (katab+u)	"He wrote it/him"
katabtu (katab+t+u)	"I write it/him"
katablu (katab+l+u)	"He wrote to it/him"
katabt*i*lu (katab+t+l+u)	"I wrote to it/him"

Iraqi Arabic

kitaba (kitab+a)	"He wrote it/him"
kitabta (kitab+t+a)	"I wrote it/him"
kitabla (kitab+l+a)	"He wrote to it/him"
kitab*i*tla (kitab+t+l+a)	"I wrote to it/him"

QUESTIONS

3.   State the rule(s) required to describe each Arabic dialect.

4.   Compare these native language rules with the rules you arrived at to describe the speakers' interlanguage forms in Part One. Concerning the possibility of language transfer, what conclusions can you draw from this comparison?

===== **Part Three** =====

There are exceptions to the generalizations noted in Part One for the English production by Egyptian Arabic speakers. Consider the data below:

[izbilaʃ]	splash
[siwetar]	sweater
[silayd]	slide
[istirit]	street
[izbilendid]	splendid
[iski]	ski
[izbasyal]	special
[istadi]	study

QUESTIONS

5.   Which of the sequences of consonants above appear to be exceptions? Which conform to the generalization you found in Part One?

6.   What interlanguage generalization can you formulate to describe these exceptions?

7.   In light of these latter data, reconsider your answer to Question 4 in terms of possible language transfer. Justify any changes or nonchanges you make.

PROBLEM 4.2

FINAL CONSONANTS

Native Language:	Spanish (Part One), Chinese (Mandarin) (Part Two)
Target Language:	English
Data Source:	Four types of recorded data: (a) reading of word lists; (b) creation of a word based on one shown to subjects and using a particular type of morpheme (e.g., comparative, superlative); (c) modified cloze reading; (d) solving of a riddle or logical anecdote.
Learner Information:	
Age:	Adults
Learning Environment:	ESL Program, U.S.
Proficiency Level:	High-intermediate and advanced

Part One

Below are examples of interlanguage forms produced by two speakers of Spanish:

Subject 1		Subject 2	
IL Phonetic Form	Gloss	IL Phonetic Form	Gloss
[bɔp]	Bob	[bɔp]	Bob
[bɔbi]	Bobby	[bɔbi]	Bobby
[rɛt]	red	[rɛθ/rɛð]	red
[rɛðər]	redder	[rɛðər]	redder
[bik]	big	[bik/ big / biɣ]	big
[wɛt]	wet	[wɛt]	wet
[wɛtər]	wetter	[wɛtər]	wetter
[bɛd]	bed	[bɛt]	bed
[pɪg]	pig	[pig]	pig
[bigər/biɣər]	bigger	[smuθ]	smooth
[bref]	brave	[smuðər]	smoother
[brevər]	braver	[rav]	rob
[prawt]	proud	[ravər]	robber
[prawdəst]	proudest	[du]	do
[sik]	sick	[riðu]	redo
[sikəst]	sickest	[bek]	bake
[fris]	freeze	[priβek]	prebake
[son]	zone	[sef]	safe
[fʌsi]	fuzzy	[sefəst]	safest
[ðə]	the	[ðə]	the
[faðər]	father	[ðis]	this
[tæg]	tag	[bæd]	bad

67

QUESTIONS

1.   For each subject, describe the phonetic alternations in these data.

2.   What are the underlying forms that you would posit to account for these data?

3.   Provide an interlanguage generalization to account for the data for each of these subjects.

======   **Part Two**   ======

Below are examples of interlanguage forms produced by two speakers of Mandarin Chinese:

Subject 1		Subject 2	
IL Phonetic Form	Gloss	IL Phonetic Form	Gloss
[tæg/tægə]	tag	[ænd/ændə]	and
[rab/rabeə]	rob	[hæd/hædə]	had
[hæd/hæsə]	had	[tɔb/tɔbə]	tub
[hiz/hizə]	he's	[staDɪd/staDɪdə]	started
[smuðə]	smoother	[fiʊd/fiʊdə]	filled
[rayt]	right	[bɪg/bɪgə]	big
[dɛk]	deck	[rɛkənayzdə]	recognized
[zɪp]	zip	[ɪz/ɪzə]	is
[mɪs]	miss	[sɛz/sɛzə]	says
[wɛt]	wet	[wɔtə]	water
[dɪfər]	differ	[afə]	after
[ovər]	over	[lidə]	leader
[bigər]	bigger		
[kɪkɪn]	kicking		
[tæpɪn]	tapping		
[lebər]	label		
[lɛtər]	letter		
[blidɪn]	bleeding		
[lidə]	leader		

QUESTIONS

4.   For each subject, describe the phonetic alternations in these data.

5.   What are the underlying forms that you would posit to account for these data?

6.   Provide an interlanguage generalization to account for the data for each of these subjects.

7.   The generalization needed for the L2 data from the Chinese speakers is not found in other languages. How can you account for the fact that a second language learner has created a rule that is not "natural," that is, one that is not found in other languages? (Hint: Chinese has no word final obstruents. Do you need word final voiced obstruents as part of the underlying form?)

PROBLEM 4.3

PRODUCTION/PERCEPTION 1

Native Language: Japanese
Target Language: English
Data Source: Perception and production of stimulus items
Learner Information:

    Age: 19 - 31 (average = 26)
    Age of First Exposure: 13
    Learning Environment: Foreign language classroom and naturalistic exposure in the U.S.
    Proficiency Level: "Good" (5 learners)
    "Poor" (1 learner)

LINGUISTIC BACKGROUND

In Japanese, there is just one liquid phoneme, transcribed phonemically as /r/. It has been described as a "loose alveolar stop" that often sounds like /d/ to Americans. It can be produced with lateral articulation, usually with a tendency toward retroflexing. In English, /r/ is realized phonetically as an alveolar approximant that may or may not be retroflex. American /l/ is realized as a lateral alveolar approximant. Of most importance is that Japanese has no distinctive contrast between the liquid phonemes, whereas English does. Moreover, Japanese has constraints that preclude both [stop + liquid] consonant clusters and liquids in syllable-final and word-final positions.

METHODOLOGICAL BACKGROUND

Six native speakers of Japanese and four native speakers of American English each recorded 96 English stimuli (two tokens each of 48 items). One month following the recordings, a perception test was administered. The perception test consisted of listening to the subject's own recordings along with those of the other subjects. Subjects responded by writing the word they heard.

======= **Part One** =======

The following stimulus materials were presented to the learners:

Test words (repeated twice, 64 tokens)

Initial	Consonant Cluster	Medial	Final
read-lead	breed-bleed	mirror-miller	dear-deal
room-loom	broom-bloom	berry-belly	core-coal
road-load	grow-glow	correct-collect	war-wall

Fillers (repeated twice, 32 tokens)

Initial	Vowel	Medial	Final
deep-keep	boat-boot	swimming-swinging	him-hip
hope-soap	get-got	defend-descend	mad-man

RESULTS

Identification errors (expressed as a percentage of opportunities)

	Productions by		
	Native English Speakers	Native Japanese Speakers (good)	Japanese Speakers (poor)
English n = 4	1 (1)	1	35
Japanese (good) n = 5	11	10 (7)	34
Japanese (poor) n =1	26	28	(34)

Rows indicate groups of subjects as listeners. Columns indicate groups of subjects as speakers. The numbers in ( ) indicate the percent errors in identification by each subject on his/her own production, averaged across subjects. This number reflects the average self-perception (in the case of the Japanese-poor, only one subject is involved).

QUESTIONS

1. Describe the pattern shown in the table above.

2. Compare the production of good Japanese speakers (as judged by native speakers of English) with their perception of words pronounced by English speakers. What do these data suggest about the relationship between production and perception of /l/ and /r/?

3. Compare the perception that good Japanese speakers have of their own performance with (a) their perception of the other good Japanese learners' performance, and (b) their perception of the native English speakers' performance. What do these comparisons tell us about self-perception?

4. Compare the perception that good Japanese speakers have of their own performance with the perception that the native speakers of English have of the good Japanese speakers. What does this comparison tell us about self-perception?

=========   **Part Two**   =========

The relationship between production and perception by individual Japanese subjects (errors expressed as a percentage of opportunities)

		Perception of productions by		
Japanese	Perception by native judges (production by Japanese)	Self	English speakers	Other Japanese (good)
1	0	17	19	21
2	1	6	17	16
3	0	2	7	7
4	1	3	6	5
5	3	5	5	3
6	35	34	26	28

The second column (perception by English speaking judges) reports the overall percent errors in identification by the four English speaking listeners. The other columns report perception errors for each Japanese subject on his/her own productions, the four English productions, and the other productions by the good Japanese producers', excluding his/her own productions.

QUESTIONS

5.   Consider the errors made by Japanese nonnative speakers in perception (Columns 3-5) and in production (Column 2). To what extent is their performance comparable in perception and in production? Describe the differences among subjects.

=========   **Part Three**   =========

Average errors in identification (expressed as a percentage of opportunities) by the five Japanese speakers categorized as "good" on productions by English speakers and other good Japanese, divided according to word position

Word position	Productions by Native English speakers /r/ /l/		Japanese (good) /r/ /l/	
Initial	4	18	6	10
Consonant Cluster	26	9	23	5
Medial	13	14	9	13
Final	2	2	8	3

QUESTIONS

6.   Based on the distribution of perception errors made by Japanese speakers, what are the most difficult contexts for the identification of /l/-/r/ contrasts?

7.   Suggest an explanation for the asymmetric development of perception and production abilities revealed by these data.

*8.   How would traditional Contrastive Analysis deal with this pattern of difficulty?

PROBLEM 4.4

PRODUCTION/PERCEPTION 2

Native Language: Mandarin, Taiwanese
Target Language: English
Data Source: Reading aloud, listening task
Learner Information:
  Age: Listeners: adults
  Talkers: adults and children
  Age of First Exposure: Adults: after the age of 20
  Children: 7;6 (average)
  Learning Environment: Naturalistic exposure in the U.S.
  Length of Residence: Adults: 1.1; 5.1
  Children: 12

METHODOLOGICAL BACKGROUND

Four groups of "talkers" produced test sentences that were then rated for foreign accent by the "listeners."

(1)   Native speakers of Taiwanese (average length of residence in U.S. was 1.1 years) who had begun learning English as adults. (Taiwan-1)

(2)   Native speakers of Taiwanese (average length of residence in U.S. was 5.1 years) who had begun learning English as adults. (Taiwan-5)

(3)   Native speakers of Taiwanese who had begun learning English in the U.S. as children (average age was 7;6 years). These subjects had lived an average of 12 years in the U.S. (Children)

(4)   Native speakers of American English.

The test sentences all contain sounds not present in the native languages of these subjects. The sentences are given below:

> The good shoe fits Sue.
> I can read this for you.
> The red book was good.

Three groups of listeners rated these sentences for foreign accent.

(1)   A subset of the subjects in Taiwan-1 above (average years in U.S.= 1.5 years).
(2)   A subset of the subjects in Taiwan-5 above (average years in U.S.= 5.3 years).
(3)   Native speakers of American English.

The listeners listened to randomized sentences produced by the talkers and were told to estimate the degree of foreign accent in each sentence.

Figure 1 shows the way the three listener groups rated sentences produced by the four groups of talkers.

Figure 1: Ratings by three listener groups of four talker groups (maximum score = 256)

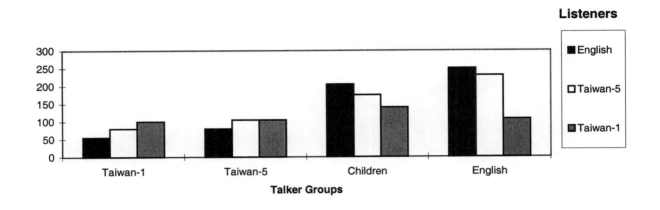

QUESTIONS

1.   Consider the way native speakers evaluate the three groups of learners. Are they able to distinguish degrees of foreign accent? Is Taiwan-5 (the longer residence group) able to make these distinctions? Is Taiwan-1 (the shorter residence group) able to make these distinctions?

2.   Given these data, what is the relationship between exposure to a second language and the ability to perceive a foreign accent?

3.   Now consider the same learners as talkers. Describe the differences between the shorter residence learners and the longer residence learners in terms of how their pronunciation is perceived.

4.   How would you interpret the relationship between perception and production shown by these data?

5.   Look at the judgments about the accent of Taiwanese speakers who had learned English as children. How would you account for the fact that their accent was not rated as "native" as the accent of native English speakers?

*6.   There is no statistically significant difference between the perception by Native English speakers of Taiwan-1 and Taiwan-5. What does this suggest about the relationship between length of residence and one's ability to acquire second language pronunciation?

SECTION FIVE

Variation

================= **PROBLEM 5.1** =================

NARRATIVES

Native Language:	Arabic (Parts I and II), Italian (Parts III and IV)
Target Language:	English
Data Source:	Oral report of a movie "Little Man, Big City" (Parts I and III), written report of the same movie (Parts II and IV)
Learner Information:	
Age:	Adult
Learning Environment:	ESL classroom
Proficiency Level:	Intermediate

========== **Part One** ==========

DATA

    I saw today a movie about a man in a big city. I want to tell you about a movie, my friend. The movie began with a man about 40 years old or 45 in his apartment in the city and he was disturbed by alarm clock, TV, and noisy outside the house or outside the apartment and he woke up in a bad temper and he wanted a fresh air, he went when he opened the window to get this fresh air, he found a smoke, smoke air, dirty air. The movie also showed that the man not only disturbed in his special apartment or special house, but in everything, in work, in street, in transportation, even in the gardens and seashores. Man in the city has to wake up very early to go to the work and he has to as the movie shows, he has to use any means of transportation, car, bus, bicycle and all the streets are crowded, and he has no no choice or alternatively to use and he is busy day and night. At day, he has to work hard among the machines, the typewriters and among papers, pencils and offices in the city. And when he wanted to take a rest in his house or outside his house in the garden or the seashore.... He can't because the seats are crowded with people. When he wanted to take a meal in restaurant, the restaurant is crowded, everything is crowded in the city and very, very it' s not good place or good atmosphere to to live in. The movie showed that. And the man began to feel sick and thus he wanted to consult the doctors to describe a medicine or anything for for health, but the doctors also disagreed about his illness or they couldn't diagnose his illness correctly. This they show at first. Want to make us know about the life in the city. The man began to think about to find a solution or answer for this dilemma. OK dilemma? Dilemma. He thought that why not to go to the open lands and to build houses and gardens and and to live in this new fresh land with fresh air and fresh atmosphere and why don't we stop smoking in the factories by using filters, filters and stop smoking from the cars and all industrial bad survivals or like smoking like dirty airs and so on. The man also wanted to make kids or childrens in the houses not to play or to use sports inside houses, but to go outside the houses in the garden and to play with balls, basket anything. They like to play. And also he wanted to live in a quiet and calm apartment. People inside houses must not use TV in a bad way or a noisy way. Must use it in a calm way or in a quiet way and that, I think, that is a good solution or a good answer for this city dilemma.

QUESTIONS

1.   Categorize the data by separating this speaker's use of the present tense from his use of the past tense. Continue the model format as set up as follows:

Past	*Present*
I saw today a movie about a man in a big city.	I want to tell you about a movie, my friend.
The movie began with a man about 40 years old or 45 in his apartment in the city and he was disturbed by alarm clock, TV,…	

77

2.   Focusing on tense shifts, from past to present and vice versa, work out an interlanguage generalization that might account for this shift.

=========== **Part Two** ===========

DATA

I saw a movie about a man in a city (big city). I want to tell you what I saw and what is my opinion. The movie began with a man about 40 years old, in his apartment in a big city. He was disturbed by many things like Alarm O' Clock, T.V., Radio and noisy outside. He want a fresh air, but he could not because the city is not a good place for fresh air. There are many factories which fill the air with smoke. The movie showed the daily life of a man in the city. He is very busy day and night. He had to go to his work early by any means of transportation, car, bus, bicycle. The streets are crowded, everything in the city is crowded with people, the houses, streets, factories, institutions and even the seashores. Man in a big city lives a hard and unhealthy life, noisy, dirt air, crowded houses and smoke are good factors for sickness. The man in the big city tried to find answer to this dilemma. Instead of living in crowded, unhealthy places, he wanted places that must be used for living. People must live in good atmosphere climate and land. Gardens, which are good places for sports, must surround houses. My opinion is that man' s solution for the problem is good and acceptable especially for health.

QUESTIONS

3.   Categorize the data by separating this speaker's use of the present tense from his use of the past tense, as in Part One:

4.   Focusing on tense shifts, from past to present and vice versa, work out an interlanguage generalization that might account for this shift.

5.   Account for the similarities/differences between this Arabic learner's tense shifting in written discourse as opposed to the oral version. Provide examples detailing your explanations.

=========== **Part Three** ===========

DATA

So it there was a movie, um probably filmed some years ago in Budapest . . . from . . . it was a Hungarian? a Hungarian film. It was a cartoon, and it dealt with modern life in the big city. The man who uh well the.... It is a description of the life of a man in a big city. From morning when he wakes up and go to work with many other people all living in the same . . . under the same circumstances and uh with the same paternistic form in the big city. And from a very common description of life of modern life, of our pressure, of our stress, of our anxieties and of all the um possible uh limits and uh rules we have to follow living in a big city. And it deals with uh it dealt with pollution problems in a town, in a city where industry and uh residential areas are very close together. And . . . the moral of the story is uh that if people could do something all together the population would have the courage and the will to do eh something for . . . to deal with these problems that may reasonably be able to find a solution or to encourage authorities to face the problem and . . . to find solutions to the . . . to it, because it's not so difficult in fact.

QUESTIONS

6.   Categorize the data by separating this speaker's use of the present tense from his use of the past tense. Follow the format set up in Part One.

7.   Focusing on tense shifts, from past to present and vice versa, work out an interlanguage generalization that might account for this shift.

<hr>

=======   **Part Four**   =======

DATA

The film dealt mainly with problems concerning our modern life in a big city. The main character of the story is an ordinary man living and working in the city. The film describes his everyday life and shows him in the different moments of a typical working day. In doing this the author of the story tell us about general very common problems of a modern city, where "civilization," industrialization and the consequent need for more apartment buildings, have brought to serious damages to the environment. A city, therefore, where people do not live, but vegetate; where it is hard to find peace and loneliness; where pollution constantly endangers our health. Towards the end, however, the author suggests the possibility of finding solutions and bringing improvements to the present condition through the active participation of citizens in dealing with the matter.

<hr>

QUESTIONS

8.   Categorize the data by separating this speaker's use of the present tense from his use of the past tense, as in Part One.

9.   Focusing on tense shifts, from past to present and vice versa, work out an interlanguage generalization that might account for this shift. Account for the similarities and differences between this learner's tense shifting in written discourse as opposed to the oral version. Provide examples detailing your explanation.

10.   What similarities and differences do you find between the Arabic speaker's description of the film (Parts One and Two) and the Italian speaker's description of the same film (Parts Three and Four)? How do you account for these?

PROBLEM 5.2

ORAL INTERVIEW

Native Language:	Teochew (a dialect of Chinese)
Target Language:	English
Data Source:	Oral interview
Learner Information:	
Age:	Adult
Age of First Exposure:	6
Learning Environment:	Primary school in Singapore where English was the medium of instruction

---

Interview between Singaporean waitress and a native speaker of English.

HP: Interviewer
N: Singaporean waitress

      HP   What school did you go to?
      N   Around my parent staying, Perryman Secondary School. There's number of schools there. There's also got churches there.
      HP   Mmm
5   N   Catholic churches there.
      HP   Are you a Catholic?
      N   I am Methodist.
      HP   Tell me about your school.
      N   Is small. Geylang Methodist School is called.
10 HP   Ahem
      N   From Primary One to Secondary. Then I transfer myself to Tomlin (?) School. Is government school.
      HP   Were your lessons in English or in Chinese?
      N   We speak English.
15 HP   Are there many schools where you speak only Chinese?
      N   Chinese? Ya, is. My place there I got one, Kong Kong Yang School.
      HP   Did you learn Chinese at school?
      N   Ya - only as subject.
      HP   Did they teach any Malay at your school?
20 N   Ah Malay - ya a few.
      HP   A few?
      N   Number ah. Depends ah. Some of them they take Malay as one dialec' and some they take two dialec', that means the Chinese and the Malay. They take two types.
25 HP   Oh I see. What about your own dialect? Are you Hokkien?
      N   No I am a Teochew.
      HP   Do you know what part of China the Teochew come from?
      N   Amoy ah! I t'ing. You ever been to China?
      HP   I've been to Hong Kong.
30 N   Hong Kong is only Cantonese. Very nice place is Hong Kong.
      HP   Do you speak Cantonese?
      N   Speak little Cantonese.
      HP   What about Hokkien?
      N   Mostly Singaporeans they understand Hokkien. All t'e other dialect they
35   learn. We mostly - we know - our home ah counted my parent. My father know English, my mother a Hokkien. So we usually mix dialect.
      HP   You mix them, do you?
      N   Mix them ah. Sometime we speak English, sometime we speak Hokkien, sometime we speak Teochew.
40 HP   Tell me a bit more about your school. When you went to Primary School

		did you get religious instruction?
	N	Ya, we have. When I am schooling in Primary Two to Six we studying mostly from bibles. Actually from Primary One we don't do that lah. We jus' - we get lesson about scripture. So we studying we sing songs
45		- sometime we learn gospel.
	HP	Do you attend a Methodist Church?
	N	Ya. I go every Sunday to Methodist Church.
	HP	Are your ministers Chinese?
	N	I go to Chinese Church when I was small. Hm. English I go now.
50	HP	Are some of the ministers, the pastors in your church from Australia or America or are they local people?
	N	Mos'ly from Australia - some local. Some of them they tell us abou' their life. Some they live in other par' of world.

....

	HP	Where do you go when you go out?
55	N	I go ou' - I mos'ly with some friend'. Usually two or three we wen' to pi'ni' and then walk aroun' towns...
	HP	And when you go with your family - where would you go?
	N	Usually we go t'dinner in restaurant - we go to Chinese restaurant. All my family go.
60	HP	What sort of things would you eat?
	N	Oh we usually go to Chinese restaurant. They usually have dishes on big tray- round tray. Have soup, have prawn, mee. You know mee ah?
	HP	Yes, I like mee.
	N	Two three month back I have dinner with a group of friend ah. We
65		wen' to a - you know where is ah -Hoices? Ya Karang National building. There's a number of coffee houses there. Chinese porridge.
	HP	How do you make Chinese porridge?
	N	Rice - they use rice.
	HP	And how do they make it?
70	N	They add more water than usual. Jus' add more water on rice, then you cook- then become porridge.
	HP	Do you eat it with sugar?
	N	No. Depends on what type of things you eat. Some of them they have pork and spice.
75	HP	And do you eat that in the morning?
	N	Morning - usually some of them have. Chinese custom - they usually have this.

....

	HP	Tell me a bit more about your parents. Do they come from China?
	N	My mum's parent they come from China. My other grandmother is
80		a Baba Teochew - you know baba?
	HP	She was born in Singapore.
	N	Ya, Singapore. My grandmother she speak Teochew an' she speak Malay, Baba Malay.Sometimes she wear sarong.
	HP	What do you speak to your grandmother?
85	N	I speak Teochew. To my paren' I speak Teochew an' Hokkien and sometime English.
	HP	And with your sisters?
	N	We speak mostly English.
	HP	And do both your parents understand English?
90	N	Ya. My father know to speak but my mother do not.
	HP	But she can understand English?
	N	Can understand - yes. Little bit.
	HP	What does your father do?
	N	My father - I am not very sure. He use to connec' radio - to make sound
95		- but I am not very sure.

	HP	Does your mother work?
	N	Housewife.
	HP	Is it very common for Singapore women to go out and work?
	N	It is very common nowadays.
100	HP	You talked about your sisters before. What about brothers? Do you have brothers?
	N	Ya, have
	HP	How many?
	N	Two youngers and one elders. One elders wen' to Bermuda - is
105		in Canada.
	HP	For how long?
	N	Half a year.
	HP	Does he intend to come back?
	N	Coming back - ya - not very sure. Maybe he stay there.
110	HP	How does he like it there?
	N	He say - is quite different from Singapore. Thing there is much more expensive than here. An' robber there - lot of robber an' thieves.
	HP	What town did you say?
	N	Bermuda.
115	HP	Bermuda - in the West Indies?
	N	I don't know. Think is Canada.
	HP	What about your two younger brothers?
	N	Two youngers are - one is waiting for army an other one is study.
	HP	What about you - do you want to stay in Singapore?
120	N	This I am not very sure myself.
	HP	What about holidays? Do you have some weeks off each year?
	N	Holidays - we seldom get them. We don' get holiday.
	HP	After you've worked here for one year - do you get one week off?
	N	I haven't get one. I work here two year. Last year, due to the business
125		I get no holiday.
	HP	What about Chinese New Year. Do you get any time off then?
	N	Ya, have four day off.
	HP	Does everybody close down on Chinese New Year?
	N	Yes - mos' shop -Mos' Chinese shop - but for the Malay and the Indians I
130		think some of them open.
	HP	When is the Chinese New Year?
	N	This year - I think is February - not very sure myself. Depend on the moon.
	HP	Do you get a day off for National Day?
135	N	National Day? Here I think we open.
	HP	What happens on National Day?
	N	Depends. They sing song and they make speeches. The minister he announce what time the prime minister will come. Not very sure myself, you see.

QUESTIONS

1.   Identify nonstandard features in this learner's interlanguage. For example, pay attention to:
   - subject pronouns
   - morphology (person, number, tense)
   - negation
   - articles
   - word order

2.   Of the features you have identified, which is most systematic? Which is the most variable? What factors do you use in deciding what is systematic and what is variable?

3.   From your knowledge of other learner data, are these interlanguage features due to transfer or to developmental processes? How can you decide?

4.   Discuss the concept of fossilization in light of these data.

SECTION SIX

Oral Language

PROBLEM 6.1

COMPREHENSIBILITY

Native Language:	Mixed
Target Language:	English
Data Source:	Native speaker ratings of nonnative speakers' readings of sentences
Learner Information:	
Age:	Adults
Learning Environment:	ESL learners
Number of subjects:	14 Nonnative speakers
	27 Native speaker raters

Part One

METHODOLOGICAL BACKGROUND

Native speakers of English were presented with 28 sentences read orally. They were asked to rate each sentence according to the pronunciation (good or bad).

DATA

Sentence	Number of responses		Read by subj. no.
	Good	Bad	
1. Nowhere can you see so many people.	26	1	13
2. An active president has chosen our country.	7	20	9
3. His behavior will lead to go to prison.	6	21	10
4. He does spend his holidays always at home.	2	25	2
5. I am waiting until I find a rich man.	24	3	14
6. He is unusual to have a new car.	8	19	1
7. He said that he no money has.	3	24	6
8. My nephew grew up while he was in college.	15	12	4
9. It is unusual for him to have a new car.	26	1	1
10. He doesn't write good books.	22	5	7
11. He said that he has no money.	25	1	6
12. His behavior will lead him to prison.	3	24	10
13. Our country has chosen an active president.	17	10	9
14. We had to water the garden because it didn't rain yesterday.	0	27	3
15. I prevented him to going with me.	2	25	12
16. I am sorry that he was disappointed.	27	0	8
17. It is necessary for finish the work.	14	13	5
18. I prevented him from going with me.	14	13	12
19. He always spends his holidays at home.	10	17	2
20. It is necessary in order to finish the work.	25	2	5
21. They are interested in riding horses.	19	8	11
22. He writes not good books.	4	23	7
23. Nowhere do you can see so many people.	26	1	13
24. We had to water the garden after it hadn't rained yesterday.	0	27	3
25. They are interested in horses riding.	19	8	11
26. I am sorry for him be disappointed.	16	11	8
27. I am waiting until find rich man.	4	17	14
28. My nephew was grown up while he was in college.	17	10	4

QUESTIONS

1.   Consider the sentences read by each individual subject. Describe the relationship between these sentences.

2.   Given the above data, which factor(s) do you think entered into decisions about the quality of nonnative speakers' pronunciation?

3.   Using the accompanying tape, rate the above sentences according to the quality of pronunciation (good or bad).

4.   To what extent do your results correspond with those given above?

===== **Part Two** =====

DATA

Below are transcriptions by a native speaker of English of the sentences in Part One. (The subject heard each sentence only once).

1.   Nowhere can you see so many people.
2.   An ectic president has chosen our country.
3.   His girlfriend will leave to go to visit.
4.   He does spend ....at home.
5.   We had to water the garden after it rained yesterday.
6.   It is unusual for have a new car.
7.   He said that he not manage this.
8.   My nephew grew up when he was in college.
9.   It is unusual for him to have a new car.
10.   He doesn't write good books.
11.   He said that he has no money.
12.   ....
13.   Our country has chosen an active president.
14.   We had......................because it didn't rain yesterday.
15.   I permitted him to going with me.
16.   I'm sorry that he was dissapointed.
17.   It is necessary for finish the work.
18.   I prevented him from going with me.
19.   Hold his pants..........his.............at home.
20.   It is necessary in order to finish the work.
21.   But am interested in riding horses.
22.   He likes not good books.
23.   Nowhere do you can see so many people.
24.   I am waiting until I find a rich man.
25.   They are interested in horses riding.
26.   I am sorry for him to be disappointed.
27   I am waiting on the fine ridge now.
28.   My nephew was grown up while he was in college.

QUESTIONS

5.   What objective criteria can you use to determine the degree of comprehensibility?

6.   Based on these criteria, order the sentences from most easy to understand to least easy to understand.

7.   Listen to the tape and make a transcription of the sentences you hear.

8.   Do the objective criteria you used in Question 5 yield the same orderings as the ordering derived from Question 6?

9.   Given the results in 6 and 8, what generalization can you make about which sentences are easiest to understand and why?

10.   In what way is comprehensibility a function of interacting factors?

PROBLEM 6.2

INPUT AND PRODUCTION

Native Language: Spanish
Target Language: English
Data Source: Conversation with a native speaker; data collected every 2 weeks over a 10-month period (Part One); data collected at 1-month intervals over an 8½-month period (Part Two)

Learner Information:
      Age: One adult (age 33)
                                 One child (age 5)
      Length of Exposure to TL: Adult-4 months
                                   Child-4 months
      Learning Environment: Naturalistic

LINGUISTIC BACKGROUND

In Spanish subject pronouns can be optionally present or absent. Thus, the following sentences are both grammatical:

    El/Ella come como una bestia.
    he/she eats like a beast
    "He/she eats like a beast."

    Come como una bestia.
    eats like a beast
    "He/she eats like a beast."

In the interlanguage of Spanish speakers, one frequently finds examples such as the following in which subject pronouns are not present:
    NS: What do you do on the weekends?
    NNS: Work in the house with my friend.

    NNS: Begins in March.

    NNS: Is low?

Part One

DATA

A = Alberto, adult

1.   NS: Ahm, Is a boy.
      A: Is a boy.
      NS: Yeah, is that a good sentence or bad sentence?
      A: Good.
      NS: Good, O.K., ahm, ahm, Is a dog.
      A: Is a dog? Good.
      NS: Good. Ahm, this apple.

2.   A: Is part (/uh/) the week.
      NS: Good. Very good. Is this a weekend?
      A: No.
      NS: No.

88

	A:	Is part of week.
	NS:	Um hum, oh, is this a week day?
	A:	No, is weekend.
	NS:	Very good, good.

3.
	A:	She is dead.
	NS:	Good.
	A:	De, dead.
	NS:	Dead, yeah.
	A:	Yeah, is dead.
	NS:	Good explanation, good sentence.
	A:	Yeah.

4.
	A:	Uh, uh no good explain.
	NS:	No good explain.

5.
	A:	Oh sure. Drink too much.
	NS:	Drink too much. What were you drinking?

6.
	A:	O any person. no, no no live more.
	NS:	No live more?
	A:	Yeah, no live, es, she, I need go and let in this funeral home.

7.
	A:	Yeah, is charm.
	NS:	Is charming or.
	A:	Yeah, is charming.
	NS:	Charming.

8.
	A:	Yesterday my country change, ah, President.
	NS:	Oh yeah? Now, is the new one a good one?
	A:	Um?
	NS:	Is a good President? Do you like him? No?
	A:	No.
	NS:	No.
	A:	Is opposite of my ideas.

9.
	A:	My country?
	NS:	No, here, no.
	A:	Here?
	NS:	Is good?
	A:	Yeah, this is good.

10.
	NS:	Come at five o'clock.
	A:	I not come, no? Is no is good?
	NS:	IS; whatever you say is good. I'm interested to see what you say.

C = Cheo, child

1.
	C:	Y/Is a boy. Y house.
	NS:	Very good.

2.
	C:	Es a house.
	NS:	Very, very good.

3.
	C:	Pu- water.
	NS:	What?
	C:	Put-t, put it water.
	NS:	Put water.
	NS:	Good. um, why is he doing that?

4.
	NS:	You want to sit on the floor?
	C:	Hum?
	NS:	You want to sit on the floor? Sit up here?

5.
	NS:	Does she speak English?
	C:	No.

NS: Nothing?
C: No.
NS: She doesn't talk? Always quiet? No talk?

6.   C: Come to a little boyses.
      NS: Hum.
      C: [making noises of being satisfied: um,um]
      NS: Is a, a pencil.
      C: Pencil.

QUESTIONS

1.   With regard to subject pronouns, focus on the kind of input the native speaker is giving the nonnative speaker. How would you characterize the input (e.g., repetition, confirmation)?

2.   In each case, who initiates the utterances that contain verbs with no subjects? In what way is this significant? That is, what evidence is there that the native speaker may be contributing to the nonnative speaker's assumption that English does not use pronouns?

=====   **Part Two**   =====

Figure 1: Subjectless Utterances in Alberto's Speech

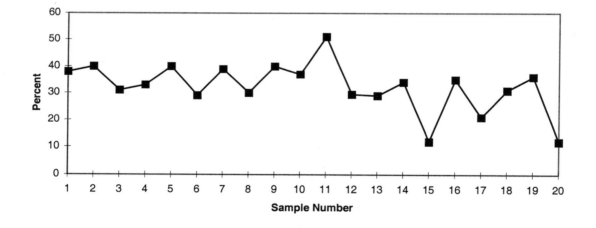

Figure 2: Subjectless Utterances in Input to Alberto

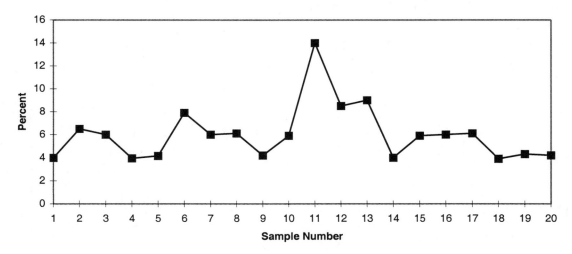

QUESTIONS

3.   Consider Figures 1 and 2. Describe the relationship between the frequency of subjectless pronouns in the input and Alberto's production of subjectless utterances. Focus, in particular, on Sample 11.

Figure 3: Subjectless Utterances in Cheo's Speech

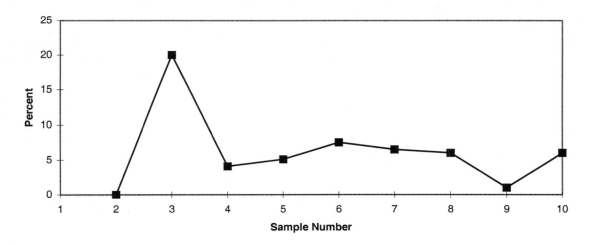

Figure 4: Subjectless Utterances in Input to Cheo

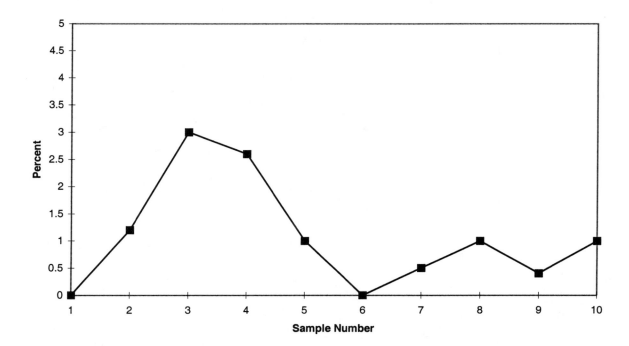

4.   Consider Figures 3 and 4. What is the relationship between the frequency of subjectless pronouns in the input and Cheo's production of subjectless utterances?

5.   Consider the sample number in which Cheo had the largest number of subjectless utterances (in Samples 1 and 2, Cheo spoke no English). How do you think this use might have been reinforced (or even initiated) by the native speaker?

════════ **PROBLEM 6.3** ════════

NNS/NNS INTERACTION

Native Language: Japanese, Spanish
Target Language: English
Data Source: Free conversation
Learner Information:
    Age: Adults
    Learning Environment: ESL in U.S. intensive program
    Proficiency Level: Intermediate
    Number of Subjects: 14 dyads

═══════ **Part One** ═══════

DATA

Listen to the tape (transcript given below).

J = native speaker of Japanese
S = native speaker of Spanish

```
J:      And your what is your mm father's job?
S:      My father now is retire
J:      retire?
S:      yes
J:      oh yeah
S:      But he work with uh uh institution
J:      institution
        [
S:      Do you know that?  The name is...some thin like eh control of the state.
J:      aaaaaaaah
S:      Do you understand more or less?
J:      State is uh...what what kind of state?
S:      (It) is uhm
J:      Michigan State?
S:      No, the the all n-n nation
                                    ]
J:      No,           government?
S:      all the nation, all the nation.  Do you know for example is a the the institution mmm of
        the state mm of Venezuela
J:      ah ah
S:      had to declare declare? nn her ingress
J:      English?
S:      No. English no (laugh)...ingress, her ingress
J:      Ingress?
S:      Ingress. yes. I N G R E S S  more or less
J:      Ingless
S:      Yes. if for example, if you, when you work you had an ingress, you know?
J:                                                          hm
J:      uh huh an ingless?
S:      yes
J:      uh huh OK
S:      yes, if for example, your homna, husband works,
J:                                                      mm
S:      when finish, when end the month his job, his boss pay--mm--him something
J:                                              hm-m   m      hm           ah-hah
```

```
S:      and your family have some ingress.  I don't know is
J:                    hm-m                        yes
J:      yes ah, OK OK
S:      more or (less) OK? and in this in this institution take care of all ingress of the
J:                    hm-m                              hm
S:      company and review the accounts
J:            hm
J:      OK I got, I see
S:      OK my father work there, but now he is old
J:                    hm     hm yea   hm
```

QUESTIONS

1.   In what ways does this conversation resemble a conversation between two native speakers? In what ways is it different?

2.   Would you characterize this conversation as one in which meaning exchange is the focus or in which understanding is the focus?

3.   What devices do these nonnative speakers use to indicate that they have not fully understood the preceding utterance?   Describe the ways in which nonunderstanding is built on nonunderstanding.

4.   To what extent are the interactional difficulties a result of pronunciation and/or perception?

=========   **Part Two**   =========

BACKGROUND INFORMATION

Nonunderstanding routines are defined as those exchanges in which there is some overt indication that understanding between participants has not been complete. An example is given below:

    NNS: When are you going to visit me?
    NNS: Pardon me?

DATA

A.   Average number of indications of nonunderstandings in 5 minutes of transcribed data.

Type of interaction	Indications of nonunderstanding
NS-NS	0.50
NS-NNS	2.75
NNS-NNS	10.29

B.   Average number of indications of nonunderstanding in 5 minutes of transcribed data from NNS-NNS dyads. (s.d. = standard deviation)

Group 1 Same language Same proficiency	Group 2 Same language Different proficiency	Group 3 Different language Same proficiency	Group 4 Different language Different proficiency
4 dyads avg. = 4.75 s.d. = .50	3 dyads avg. = 10.67 s.d. = 3.79	4 dyads avg. = 11.25 s.d. = 2.99	3 dyads avg. = 16.00 s.d. = 3.00

QUESTIONS

5.   Consider the data in A. How would you account for the differences found among the three different kinds of conversational dyads?

6.   Consider the data in B. What explanation can you give for the differences among the four groups of nonnative speakers?

PROBLEM 6.4

COOPERATIVE DISCOURSE

Native Language:	Japanese (Part One); Japanese, Spanish (Part Two); English (Part Three)
Target Language:	English
Data Source:	Picture description task
Learner Information:	
Age:	Adults
Learning environment:	Intensive English program in U.S.
Gender:	Female/female (Part One)
	Female/male (Part Two)
	Female/female (Part Three)

METHODOLOGICAL BACKGROUND

These data come from a picture description task in which one speaker described the picture below to another who did not have visual access to the picture. The other speaker attempted to draw the picture.

====== **Part One** ======

QUESTIONS

1.   Transcribe the first interaction (or a subset) from the tape. Analyze the conversation in terms of negotiation. Find specific instances of meaning negotiation and describe them.

2.   What evidence is there of cooperation? What do the participants do to make communication easier?

3.   Give examples of self-corrections, confirmation checks, and comprehension checks. What functions do they serve?

Problem 6.4

════════ **Part Two** ════════

QUESTIONS

4.   Transcribe the second interaction (or subset) from the tape. Compare this transcription with that from Part One. Determine if negotiation takes place in the same way. Who initiates negotiation?

5.   Find examples of self-corrections, confirmation checks, and comprehension checks.

6.   What evidence is there of cooperation? Determine if there are differences in the degree to which each leads the conversation.

════════ **Part Three** ════════

QUESTIONS

7.   Make a tape of two native speakers (of English or of some other language) undertaking the same task as in Parts One and Two. Transcribe this conversation (or a subset) and compare it with those from Parts One and Two. In what ways does the structure of this one differ from the preceding ones (e.g., pauses, hesitations, corrections, negotiations, length, accuracy)?

PROBLEM 6.5

MISUNDERSTANDING 2

Native Language:	Arabic, Spanish
Target Language:	English
Data Source:	Telephone interviews
Learner Information:	
Age:	Adults
Proficiency Level:	Low level and high level

METHODOLOGICAL BACKGROUND

The data come from telephone conversations in which a nonnative speaker was conducting an interview about food and nutrition. Nonnative speakers made telephone calls to people selected randomly from the telephone directory (all native speakers of English). The callers began each telephone call by introducing themselves, explaining that they were from the university conducting a survey for a class project on nutrition. Each caller followed the script below. After the responses to Questions 3 and 7, the callers were instructed to ask for clarification by saying *"pardon me."* A native speaker control group was also included.

Script
1. What did you eat for dinner tonight/last night?
2. Is that a typical dinner for you?
3. There has been a lot of talk lately about additives and preservatives in food. In what ways has this changed your eating habits? ....Pardon me?
4. How often do you eat at restaurants?
5. What sort of restaurants do you usually go to?
6. How often do you go shopping for food?
7. How have increasing food costs changed your eating habits?....Pardon me?
8. One last question please: Were you born and raised in the United States?

=== **Part One** ===

DATA

The data in Table 1 indicate differences in the amount of the response that is repaired after each of the two *pardon me*'s (Questions 3 and 7). The amount of response is determined by how much of the initial response is elaborated on after the *pardon me* (based on a word count).

Table 1. Percentage repaired

	% repaired	
	Question 3	Question 7
NS		
1	53.97	48.94
2	68.78	49.62
average	61.38	49.28
s.d.	10.47	.48
High Level		
1	66.71	85.43
2	74.83	87.16
3	57.67	75.56
4	44.75	77.00
average	60.99	81.29
s.d.	12.90	5.85
Low Level		
1	66.63	88.86
2	68.75	74.50
3	63.13	78.76
4	76.50	60.00
average	70.63	75.53
s.d.	4.24	11.98

QUESTIONS

1.   Describe the differences between the native speakers, the low level, and the high level groups. Focus on the differences among the three groups in terms of the patterns from Question 3 to Question 7.

2.   To what do you attribute the differences?

Part Two

DATA

Example 1 (High-level Arabic)

NNS: There has been a lot of talk lately about additives and preservatives in food. In what ways has this changed your eating habits?

NS: Uh,...well, I guess it hasn't changed too much uh, my eating habits. I try and avoid a lot of uh, sugary substances but I don't, I don't really care too much about whether it has preservatives or additives in it.

NNS: Pardon me?

NS: ...Pardon?

NNS: Pardon me, uh, what did you say?

NS: Oh, oh I said I, I don't care too much whether it has additives or preservatives in, in the food itself, uh, as long as I'm eating somewhat uh, balanced diet from a number of food groups I'm, I don't care if, if my bread has a little bit of preservative or doesn't have all the whole wheat, I don't really care that much. (laughs)

Example 2 (High-level Spanish)

NNS: How have increasing food costs changed your eating habits?
NS: You know, you like you stock up when things go on sale so that when the prices go up you don't have to uh, buy them.
NNS: Pardon me?
NS: You stock up on the uh, sale items occur so that when they go off sale you already have a bunch of it so that you don't have to go out and buy it at a higher price.

Example 3 (Low-level Spanish)

NNS: How have increasing food costs changed your eating habits?
NS: Well, we don't eat as much beef as we used to. We eat more chicken, and uh, pork, and uh, fish, things like that.
NNS: Pardon me?
NS: We don't eat as much beef as we used to. We eat more chicken and uh, uh pork and fish....We don't eat beef very often. We don't have steak like we used to.

Example 4 (Low-level Arabic)

NNS: There has been a lot of talk lately about additives and preservatives in food. In what ways has this changed your eating habits?
NS: I try to stay away from nitrites.
NNS: Pardon me?
NS: Uh, from nitrites in uh like lunch meats and that sort of thing. I don't eat those.

QUESTIONS

3.   Describe the way the response after the *pardon me* is an elaboration of the utterances immediately preceding the *pardon me.*

4.   Following is a comparison of the results of the instances of elaborated responses between the two proficiency groups and the native speaker group (after each of the two *pardon me*'s in Questions 3 and 7). To what do you attribute these differences?

Table 2. Percentage of elaborated responses (based on a word count)

NS Questions		High Level learners Questions		Low Level learners Questions	
3	7	3	7	3	7
21.00	23.00	40.00	51.61	44.12	34.38

========= **Part Three** =========

DATA

Example 1 (Low-level Arabic)

NNS: How have increasing food costs changed your eating habits?
NS: Well, I don't know that it's changed them. I try to adjust.
NNS: Pardon me?
NS: I don't think it's changed my eating habits.

Example 2 (Low-level Spanish)

NNS: There has been a lot of talk lately about additives and preservatives in food. In what ways has this changed your eating habits?
NS: Uh, I don't eat that many foods with preservatives, anyway, even before all the talk.
NNS: Pardon me?
NS: I don't eat uh, canned foods or foods that have preservatives.

Example 3 (Low-level Spanish)

NNS: There has been a lot of talk lately about additives and preservatives in food. In what ways has this changed your eating habits?
NS: Uh, I avoid them, I d-, I don't buy prepackaged foods uh, as much....Uh, I don't buy...say...potato chips that have a lot of flavoring on them....And uh, I eat better. I think.
NNS: Pardon me?
NS: ummm, pardon me? I, I eat better, I think. I, I don't buy so much food that's prepackaged.

Example 4 (High-level Spanish)

NNS: How have increasing food costs changed your eating habits?
NS: Um, I maybe I cut down some.
NNS: Pardon me?
NS: I cut down some on eating.

Example 5 (High-level Spanish)

NNS: How have increasing food costs changed your eating habits?
NS: Oh, rising costs we've cut back on the more expensive things. Gone to cheaper foods.
NNS: Pardon me?
NS: We've gone to cheaper foods.

Example 6 (High-level Arabic)

NNS: There has been a lot of talk lately about additives and preservatives in food. In what ways has this changed your eating habits?
NS: ...things that are healthier for us.
NNS: Pardon me?
NS: She'll buy things that are more healthy for us.

Example 7 (High-level Arabic)

> NNS: How have increasing food costs changed your eating habits?
> NS: Not a bit
> NNS: Pardon me?
> NS: Not one bit

Example 8 (High-level Arabic)

> NNS: How have increasing food costs changed your eating habits?
> NS: Well, it doesn't, hasn't really.
> NNS: Pardon me?
> NS: It hasn't really changed them.

Example 9 (High-level Arabic)

> NNS: How have increasing food costs changed your eating habits?
> NS: Uh well that would I don't think they've changed 'em much right now, but the pressure's on.
> NNS: Pardon me?
> NS: I don't think they've changed our eating habits much as of now...

Example 10 (High-level Arabic)

> NNS: There has been a lot of talk lately about additives and preservatives in food. In what ways has this changed your eating habits?
> NS: Well, I've been a vegetarian for 6 years and I try and not eat many food additives.
> NNS: Pardon me?
> NS: I've been a vegetarian for 6 years and I try not to eat many additives. 'cept I eat fish.

QUESTIONS

5. Focus on the parts of the response after the *pardon me*. How would you characterize the type of changes that are made? Is the part of the response that is "repaired" made more or less transparent than the initial response? In what way specifically is this accomplished (e.g., syntactically, morphologically, phonologically, etc.)?

6. The data in Table 3 compare the responses among the three groups according to whether the response following *pardon me* is more or less transparent (i.e., more or less explicit) after the first *pardon me* (Question 3) as opposed to the second *pardon me* (Question 7). To what do you attribute these differences?

Problem 6.5

Table 3. Percentage of increased transparency

NS Questions		High-Level Questions		Low-Level Questions	
3	7	3	7	3	7
31.00	28.00	37.50	46.67	56.25	42.42

PROBLEM 6.6

MISCOMMUNICATION

Native Language:	Spanish
Target Language:	English
Data Source:	Telephone Conversation
Learner Information:	
Age:	Adult
Proficiency Level:	High Beginner

BACKGROUND

The data come from a telephone conversation between a native speaker who worked at a TV repair shop and a non-native speaker. The non-native speaker was given a class assignment of finding out the cost of a television. He intended to call a sales store, but when he looked one up in the Yellow Pages, he was not aware that he was calling a repair shop rather than the intended sales store.

DATA

NNS

2. Hello could you tell me about the price and size of Sylvania color TV

4. Could you tell me about price and size of Sylvania TV color

        PAUSE

6. uh 17 inch huh?

8. yeah TV color

10. OK

        SILENCE

12. uh huh

14. ah Sony please
16. or Sylvania

18. uh huh

20. OK

22. hm hm

24. hm hm

26. OK

NS
1. Hello

3. Pardon?

5. What did you want? A service call?

7. What did you want a service call? or how much to repair a TV?

9. 17 inch

11. Is it a portable?

13. What width is it? What is the brand name of the TV?
15. We don't work on Sony's.

17. Sylvania?

19. Oh, Sylvania OK. That's American made.

21. All right. Portables have to be brought in

23. And there's no way I can tell you how much it'll cost until *he* looks at it.

25. and it's a $12.50 deposit

27. and if he can fix it that applies to

104

labor and if he can't he keeps the
$12.50 for his time and effort.

28. hm hm

29. How old of a TV is it? Do you know
off hand?

30. 19 inch

31. How old of a TV is it? Is it a very
old one or only a couple years old?

32. oh, so so

33. The only thing you can do is bring
it in and let him look at it and go
from there.

34. new television please

                    SILENCE

35. Oh you want to know

how much a new television is?

36. yeah I want buy one
television.

37. Do we want to buy
one?

38. yeah

39. Is it a Sylvania?

40. Sylvania TV color

41. Well, you know even, even if we
buy 'em, we don't give much more
than $25 for 'em. By the time we
fix 'em up and sell 'em, we can't
get more than

42. hm hm

43. $100 out of 'em time we put our time
and parts in it

44. Is it 17 inch?

45. Well, I don't...the only thing I can
tell you to do is you'd have to come
have to come to the shop. I'm on the
extension at home. The shop's closed

                    SILENCE
46. 19 inch? you don't have?

47. Do we have a 19 inch?

48. yeah

49. No, I've got a 17 inch new RCA

50. OK. Thank you. Bye.

51. Bye.

QUESTIONS

1. What evidence is there of "cooperative discourse" in the above conversation? That is, do the participants seem willing to continue the conversation?

2. What evidence is there that the participants do not understand each other? How is this indicated in the conversation?

3. What does the native speaker do to make her speech more comprehensible? What does she do to suggest that she is not interested in making the speech comprehensible?

4. Analyze the conversation in terms of what is understood (i.e., common ground) and what is not understood.

5. How would you evaluate the overall success of the conversation? You can do this in terms of rapport, or in terms of overall understanding, and/or in terms of overall communication.

══ PROBLEM 6.7 ══

COMPLIMENTS

Native Language: Various
Target Language: English
Data Source: Spontaneously collected speech samples.
Learner Information:
          Age: Adults

═══ Part One ═══

QUESTIONS

1. What form do compliments generally take in English?

2. Imagine yourself complimenting one of your classmates on something he or she accomplished or is wearing. What is the anticipated response?

3. If there are speakers of languages other than English in your class, attempt to determine the form and function of compliments in their language/culture.

4. Besides an actual compliment, what is the function of compliments?

═══ Part Two ═══

DATA

1. **American female student to her Korean male classmate:**
    A: Your English is good.
    B: (little hesitation) Thank you.

2. **An American female to a Korean male at a church function:**

    A: Your pronunciation is so nice.
    B: No response--topic change

3. **Two female students, one American, one Pakistani, are sitting alone in a classroom together waiting for the other students and the professor to arrive.**

    A: Your English is fluent.
    B: No response.

4. **Two women, a native speaker and a nonnative speaker of English meet for the first time at a cocktail party. The American says:**

    A: You have such a lovely accent.
    B: No response.

5. **American female student to her Chinese female classmate:**

    A: Your blouse is beautiful
    B: Thank you.
    A: Did you bring it from China?
    B: Yeah.

106

6.   **An American male in his 30s to a Japanese female student in her 20s:**

     A: That's a nice blouse.
     B: Thank you.

7.   **At a crowded Thanksgiving dinner party for international students, A is an American male and B is a female Chinese student. Both work together for the religious organization hosting the party. A is in his mid-30s and B in her early 20s.**

     A: That's neat! (referring to a Chinese satin coat B is wearing)
     B: No response.

8.   **A is a woman in her mid-70s and the landlady of the house where B, a Korean male student has just returned from church on a Sunday and meets A in the hallway. She stops to have a chat and opens the conversation by saying:**

     A: You look very dressy today.
     B: I used to wear like this way in church (B then turned away and went to his room.)

9.   **Two Americans, a male and a female, meet a Chinese female at a traditional American holiday dinner arranged for international students by a religious organization to which all three belong. All are in their mid-20s and have met before. The American male attempts to begin a conversation with the Chinese woman by commenting on her jewelry:**

     A: What's that necklace you're wearing?
     B: It's a Chinese fan with a phoenix on it.
     A: Oh, that's neat.
     B: No response.

10.   **A and B, both females in their mid-20s, are at a noisy monthly international church lunch. Both are staff members of the church organization, but B is also a student. A is American and B is Chinese.**

     A: It's pretty. I like this sweater.
     B: Thank you.

11.   **An American female dancing teacher says to a Japanese female student of approximately the same age:**

     A: You're doing good.
     B: Thank you.

12.   **A is an elderly American woman, neighbor of B, who is a female Japanese student.**

     A: You talk good English.
     B: Thank you.
     A: You went to school to pick it up, right?
     B: Uh-huh.
     A: That's good
     B: No response.

13.   **Two female graduate students, one American, one Japanese, meet in the cafeteria. Both are in their late 20s.**

     A: This is a nice sweater. Nice color.
     B: Oh, this? I brought it from Japan.
     A: I like it. Nice color. Very nice.
     B: Thank you.

QUESTIONS

5. In each of these examples, what do you think the intent of the compliment was?

6. How do you think the nonnative speaker interpreted the compliment?

7. How do you think native speakers interpreted the lack of response (or minimal response) by the nonnative speakers?

===== **Part Three** =====

DATA

1. **Two female graduate students are looking at photos. A is American, B is Japanese. The photos are of B's family.**

   A: Your brother is handsome.
   B: Not so much.

2. **Two American female graduate students are talking.**

   A: Your son is great.
   B: Yes, I'm proud of my son.

3. **Two female Americans meet:**

   A: I like your sweater.
   B: It's so old, my sister brought it to me from Italy a long time ago.

4. **At a cocktail reception for foreign students, C has been introduced to A by her friend B. A and B are classmates. C is a friend of B's. A is an American male and C is an Asian female. B is an Asian male.**

   A: Do you know that he's the best student in the class? (Speaking about B)
   B: No, no, no, that's not true.
   A: It *is* true. You ask anyone in our class who the best student is, they'll say it's B.
   C: Yeah. He studies all the time.
   B: I study, but my results are poor.
   A: That's not true.

QUESTIONS

8. What do you notice in the way the Americans versus the non-Americans respond to compliments?

9. Imagine yourself as the respondent to the compliment in each case. How would you have responded?

10. If you were in a position to explain to a nonnative speaker the function of compliments in English, what would you say?

*11. Note that all of the data presented in this problem are spontaneously collected speech samples. Create 5 items for a DCT (see glossary) to elicit compliments.

FLUENCY

Native Language:	Chinese
Target Language:	English
Data Source:	Tape-recorded monologues and conversations
Learner Information:	
Age:	Adults
Learning Environment:	English in the U.S.

METHODOLOGICAL BACKGROUND

Audiotapes were made of subjects' responses to written and aural instructions on the following tasks: narrative and opinion. For the narrative, the first minute and a half was transcribed.

Additional data come from conversations with a native speaker in which the same learners were engaged.

TRANSCRIPTION CONVENTIONS

Micropauses (≤. .2 seconds) are indicated by a period inside a (.). Pauses of a greater length are indicated by the time period within (.5).

Filled pauses are given with a spelling approximation (e.g., uh, um).

Colons (:) are used to indicate sound stretches; sound stretches of .3 seconds or greater are counted as filled pauses and indicated by a double colon (e.g., "she::" represents the word "she" with an extended vowel of at least .3 seconds). The degree sign (°) is used before double h's (°hh) to represent in-breaths).

Laughter is indicated by the consonant "h" within (h).

Conventional punctuation (periods, commas, and question marks) is used to represent intonation rather than sentence structure. A period indicates falling intonation, such as that used in sentence-final position; a comma indicates slightly dropping intonation or a series. Question marks indicate rising intonation rather than simply questions.

Words or parts of words that are underlined indicate louder volume and greater stress than other words in the immediate environment.

The equals sign (=) indicates that a turn is latched (there is no gap between turns, but rather, one turn is connected to another turn in time). Overlapping talk is indicated by brackets.

Parentheses are used when it cannot be determined exactly what a speaker said. When the speech was completely incomprehensible (due not only to pronunciation but also to overlapping talk or background noise), a string of the letter "x" inside parentheses is used.

=====   **Part One**   =====

DATA

Subject 1

Narrative

(18.5) A boy on: the: (.5) uh:: (.) a boy on the boat, um: on the <u>river</u> (.) and a po<u>lice</u>man (.) uh:: tell him (1.5) can (.) tell him tha:t (.) uh <u>he</u> can no::t (2.3) row: the boat. °hh So uh: he:: (1.2) ask hi:m °hh (.) uh:: (.) go ther- (.8) go <u>up</u> (.) and -uh um: (2.4) pu- an::d-uh (5.8) °hh (.7) and- uh change hi:m (.) °hh uh::: row the boat. (3.2) Bu:t uh (.7) hi- his boat (.) uh:: (.8) strongs the (.) storm, an:d-uh the <u>boa:t</u> (.8) is <u>broken</u>. Um:: (5.0) uh:m (2.5) There are many

Opinion

(2.5) I believe that (.) um: (1.3) every s- (.) high school student (.) uh: lear:n (1.0) at least (uh) one foreign language (.) is <u>good</u>. (2.2) Um: (1.1) <u>first</u> uh:m (.5) we <u>usually</u> (.) uh:: (1.5) go, go foreign (.) country uh: future. If we (.) study (.) foreign language (.) um: we can use (1.8) An:d uh (2.3) uh (3.7) in my <u>country</u> (.) °hh uh: (.4) Eng- uh: in my country, °hh <u>we</u>: (.) u:se (.) <u>English</u> and-uh um:: (.3) other language (.) in the school. Uh:: (.3) for example

Subject 2

Narrative

<u>One</u> day, Fido the dog, spotted <u>two</u> boys, <u>Tim</u> and John, at a waste- (.3) at a waste (.) disposal. Tim was looking (.) at a pair of (.5) at an <u>ol:d</u> bla:ck shoe. (1.3) He <u>wanted</u> to play catch. And so <u>Tim</u> (.) <u>threw</u> the shoe (.) acro:ss to some bushes. Fido ra:n excitedly after the shoe. And <u>he</u> brought the shoe <u>back</u>. (1.3) But (.) it wasn't the old shoe it was a <u>bra:nd</u> new one. (1.0) And the o- and the <u>owner</u> came jumping. (2.0) Said (.) "<u>That's</u> my <u>shoe</u>:." (3.1) Th' two boys were flabbergasted.

Opinion

No, I- I <u>don't</u> think that <u>old</u> people should all live in an old folks home or a nursing home. I think they should be staying with their families, (.3) an:d (1.2) their <u>grand</u>children, (.) and: (.3) be <u>part</u> of their lives. I think for <u>old</u> people, (.5) living (.7) with love (1.3) makes (.3) a <u>lot</u> of difference. (1.0) It makes them feel cared for and wanted,(3.3) it makes them (2.5) <u>know</u> (1.3) the changes that are taking place in their (1.0) son:s' and daughters' lives, (.3) an' what is happening with the children,(.3) it <u>makes</u> the old people (.4) more active more aware of what's happening in the world. Rather than in a nursing home (.4) where (.8) you're <u>pay</u>ing people to look after you (9.5) and 'uh

QUESTIONS

Listen to the tapes (transcripts given above) of the monologues.

1.   Subjectively rate each monologue in terms of fluency.

1	2	3	4	5	6
NOT FLUENT					VERY FLUENT

2.   What are the main features/characteristics that contributed to your rating of each monologue?

3.   Determine if the ratings differ by monologue type. If so, how?

4.   Compare your ratings with others. In what ways were they consistent with those of others?

5.   Select one transcript and analyze it according to the following objective characteristics.

      Amount of speech/minute
      Hesitation
      Extent of vocabulary use
      Grammatical accuracy
      Repair

6.   To what extent were your subjective judgments consistent with the objective ones?

=========   **Part Two**   =========

DATA

Subject 2—Dialogue (4 minutes, 30 seconds)

NS and NNS are friends. They have known each other for 3 months.

NS: . . . <u>right</u> up until the <u>mo</u>ment (.)
                  [
NNS: Mm-hm
NS: that the party (.3)'s gonna start we feel <u>very</u> nervous.
                                            (1.3)
NS: Even in America
                                    (1)

NS: An-
          [
NNS: D'you- d'you give parties often?
                                      (.5)
NS: Eh Not <u>that</u> often. We give them: (.5) um (.) when we fee:l like we should.
NNS: Is it umm:: (.4) the same kind of party which- (.5) which was held that night?
NS: Yeah- well (.) it o:ften is.=
NNS: =In terms of numbers is it like that?
NS: In terms of numbers it's li:ke tha:t or: (.) um maybe (.) a little bit- a few more people.
NNS: <u>Less</u> people?
NS: A few mo:re.=
NNS: =A few <u>mo:re</u> people.=
NS: =If it's any <u>le:ss</u> (.) than that it starts to just be a (.) not a party. Just a y'know like a (.)
          ga:ther ing
                  [
NNS: Ga-Gather ing
                          [
NS: y'know just a few people coming over. (.8) But um (1.5) but usually (.8)
          when we have a party (1.7) not everybody knows everybody.

NNS: Mm-h m.
               [
NS: It's people who (.) we know from different places an' we invite them an' (.7)
          an]
NNS: [But I suppose it's only natural that at the start (.) when you don't know each other it's a bit
          y'know?
                                    (.3)
NS: Yea h
NNS: [N' after that, once things wa:rm up
NS: Yeah.
NNS: It's fun, y'know? An'=
NS: =Yeah.
NNS: you get to know a different personalities an'=
NS: =Yea h
NNS: [(talk) 'bout things.

NS: Yeah. But I al- also feel (.6) um: like you do, that it's (.5) I wonder- I always think there's something missing (yu h uh)

NNS: [O:h(hh)=

NS: =There should be something going on that isn't going on but (.7) but I don't know (.) uh: how to have a party that (.9) that is (.4) uh

                                                                    [
NNS: I have never had a party before.

NS: Never in your life?=
                            [
NNS: No =Never in my life.=

NS: =Really?

NNS: Yes.

(1)

NS: Ih:- i- is that because you
                                    [
NNS: Because (.) firstly I: (1.3) Perhaps it's, y'know, I-I don't know how to handle so many people?

NS: Yeah.=

NNS: =An:d getting things ready?

NS: Yeah.   Yeah.
                    [
NNS: An' things like that.

NS: It's a lot of work.

NNS: Yea:h.

NS: It- (.5) Yeah. It i s.
                        [
NNS: An' (.6) I suppose it'll be okay if I have got (.4) about six to seven people or six to ten people in the room?

NS: Mm-hm=

NNS: =And I know all of them?

NS: Mm-hm.

NNS: But (.) especially if (.) if I'm inviting people from: (.) for example from school, from work, an' y'know my old friends and then they don't know each other then (.4) I 'ave got the added task of y'know (.3)

NS: In troduce-
           [
NNS: uh- introducing one to another.

NS: Yea h. (Tha-)
           [
NNS: An' you don't know whether they will mix and they will talk or whether it will be a flop.

NS: Yeah, I know, I know. That's always   That's always
                                                          [
NNS: the fear
                                                        (.3)
NS: Yeah.
                                                        (.7)
NS: But- though (.) the- also the feeling that I had when we had this party was (.) I- I felt (.7) like (.) the: Malaysians here

NNS: Mm-hm

NS: the Malay- I mean(.7) all Malay-
                                        [
NNS: But you had only two Malays and (.) an' t-two of us.
                                                                                          [
NS: Two Malays
        and two Chinese.
        [
NNS: Two Chinese.
                                                        (.5)
NS: That's all there were here. But there were supposed to be more Malays and (.) Sharifah was supposed to come=

NNS: Mm-h m.
                    [
NS: =and uh (.) other people were supposed to come but they didn't show up. But um
        (1.2) °tch I- I felt (.) uncomfortable or nervous because I didn't know (.3) I thin:k that when-
        when you have a party here some people expect that you are going to provide a lot of foo:d
        an-(.) an' there's going to be a- a (.) mo:re. Cuz we had a (.) pretty relaxed (.3) y'kno w
                                                                                                     [
NNS: Well- well I think that people may expect (.3) but then (.6) I would
        definitely prefer something like what you had.
NS: Mm-hm.
                                                (.8)
NNS: Than a normal party where (.) you dress up an- (.) an' small talk an' (.) (hh   hh)
                                                                                            [
NS: Yeah. Yeah. Yeah.
        Well there was small talk here. I mean
                                                [
NNS: But um: (.5) small talk in the sense of (1.2) I'm
        interested in that subject (.3) and I pursued it further.
NS: Yeah.
NNS: Rather than y'know things like how are you, y'know,
NS: Yeah.
NNS: things like that.=
NS: =Yeah, that's right. Yeah.
                                                (.8)
NS: Yeah. Well   it's interesting
                        [
NNS: An' we went back wishing that (.3) tha' (.) if't had gone on further we would
        have even enjoyed it mo:re y'know.
NS: Yeah.
NNS: Not to say that it ended too soon but (.3) y'know i(t)- we would have enjoyed- it's not a party
        where (.3) you just y'know you look at you- you just look at a watch and just (.2) wondering
        when it's time to go back y'kno w. (hh)
                                           [
NS: Yeah. Do you- d'you go to (.) parties with
        Thomas (.) often or:?
NNS: Uh: (.5) as I've said the only pahties I have attended or "par:ties" as you have said (.3) °hh is
        just um:: (.) office get-together.
NS: Mm-hm.
NNS: Things like that.
NS: But in a- I don't know if it's- I don't know what that's like (.) since you know all the people
        but (.)
NNS: Mm-hm?
        [
NS: Thomas propably doesn't know all the people, does he?
                                                (.7)
NNS: Where? Here?
NS: I(f)- if you have an office get-together d oes Thomas
                                                          [
                                                   It's that because he: (.) he attends them frequently
        with me,
NS: Uh-huh.
NNS: so he kno:ws most of the p eople
                                       [
NS: So he knows them, yeah.=
NNS: =Mm:.
NS: But um: (.) when you: go: to a party like that (.8) afterwards when you're- like when you're
        going home?
NNS: Mm-hm?
NS: Do you and Thomas (.) talk abo ut
                                       [
NNS: Exchange notes
NS: Exchange notes? Yeah(h). Yeah(h).

	[[
NNS:	Yeah. Yeah. Yeah (eh heh hh)
NS:	You d(h)o that? (.5) Because Heidi and I do.

QUESTIONS

Listen to the tape transcribed above (Subject 2 of Part One).

7.   Subjectively rate the nonnative speaker dialogue in terms of the nonnative's fluency using the following scale.

1	2	3	4	5	6
NOT FLUENT					VERY FLUENT

8.   What are the main features and characteristics that contributed to your rating?

9.   How does this rating compare with the rating based on Subject 2's monologues (Part One)?

10.   Select a portion from the dialogue and analyze it according to the following characteristics (in some instances, you might want to compare the NNS's speech with the NS's, e.g., number of turns, amount of talk):

Amount of speech/minute
Amount of talk
Hesitation
Turns
Backchannels
Questions (direct and indirect)
General comprehensibility
Repair

11.   To what extent were your subjective judgments consistent with the objective ones?

SECTION SEVEN

Communication Strategies

DESCRIPTION AND CLASSIFICATION 1

=== **Part One** ===

Native Language:	English
Target Language:	French
Data Source:	Description of drawings of objects
Learner Information:	
Age:	9
Amount of Exposure:	4 years
Learning Envoronment:	French immersion
Number of Subjects:	18

DATA	NNS Description	Translation
1. **garden hose**:	Le l'eau vient de ça. C'est attaché à...	The water comes out of it. It is attached to...
2. **garden hose**:	Quelque chose qui est sur le mur et il y a un fausset avec un...	Something that is on the wall and there is a tap with a...
3. **wooden spoon**:	On l'utilise pour prendre...si on mange	You use it to make...if you eat
4. **drill**:	C'est électrique et si on veut mettre dans un...Ca tourne et ça met des...	It's electric and if you want to put into a...turns and it makes some...
5. **screwdriver**:	On utilise pour faire...Il y a des gris, des rouges. Le rouge c'est comme on met tes mains au-dessus. L'autre part ca peut faire tu mettre les...	You use it to make...there are some grey and some red. The red is like you put your hands under it. The other part is so you can make the...
6. **playpen**:	On peut mettre un bébé dedans. Il y a comme un trou.	You put a baby in it. It is like a hole.
7. **stool**:	Il ressemble comme une lettre "A."	It looks like the letter "A."
8. **rubber stamp**:	Le part brun regarde comme c'est une tête.	The brown part looks like a head.
9. **stool**:	C'est quand tu assis sur un petit, c'est comme un table.	It's when you sit on a little one, it's like a table.
10. **swing**:	C'est une sorte de, tu peux dire, chaise que quand tu "move". Des fois, c'est sur des arbres.	It's a kind of, you could say, chair for when you move. Sometimes it is in the trees.
11. **high-chair**:	C'est une sorte de chaires et il y a une plate-forme là sur. Tu mets les bébés dedans et ils mangent sur le plate-forme.	It's a kind of chair and there is a platform on it. You put babies in it and they eat on the platform.
12. **folding-chair**:	C'est une autre sorte de chaise.	It's another kind of chair.
13. **stool**:	C'est en forme de un "A".	It's in the shape of an "A."
14. **wheelchair**:	C'est une sorte de chaise pour les personnes qui ne peuvent pas marcher.	It's a kind of chair for people who cannot walk.

15. **playpen:**
    C'est comme un cage mais tu mets des   It's like a cage but you put babies in it.
    bébés là-dedans.
16. **child's car seat:**
    C'est une chaise pour bébé que tu mets   It's a chair for a baby that you put in a car to
    dans la voiture pour tu sois "safe", sauf   keep you safe. (cf. 71)
17. **garden chair:**
    C'est une chaise que tu mets dehors,   It's a chair that you put outside, in the
    dans le jardin, dans le soleil.   garden, in the sun.
18. **calculator:**
    C'est une petite machine avec des   It's a little machine with numbers.
    nombres.
19. **playpen:**
    C'est une sorte de boîte que tu mets,   It's a kind of box that you put, it is where you
    c'est où tu mets les bébés pour jouer.   put the babies to play.
20. **stool**:
    C'est une chaise en bois.   It's a wooden chair.
21. **high-chair:**
    C'est une chaise de bébés quand les   It's a chair for babies when babies eat.
    bébés mangent.
22. **wooden spoon:**
    C'est une cuiller en bois.   It's spoon of wood.
23. **spatula:**
    On l'utilise dans la cuisine si on fait des You use it in the kitchen if you make
    crêpes ou quelque choses et on veut la   pancakes or something and you want to pick
    prender, on l'utilise ça.   them up, you use this.
24. **can opener:**
    Quelque chose que tu utilises dans la   Something you use in the kitchen when you
    cuisine quand tu veux ouvrir des   want to open bottles.
    bouteilles.
25. **spatula:**
    Quelque chose que tu utilises souvent   Something that you use often for picking up
    pour enlever quelque chose.   something.
26. **hair dryer:**
    Quelque chose que tu utilises quand tes   Something that you use when your hair is
    cheveux sont mouillés et que tu veux   wet and you want to dry it.
    que ça va sec.
27. **vacuum cleaner:**
    Quelque chose que tu utilises quand tu   Something you use when you want to clean
    veux nettoyer les choses.   things.
28. **wheelchair:**
    Quelque chose que les personnes   Something that handicapped people sit in.
    handicappés assis dedans.
29. **shovel:**
    Quelque chose que tu utilises sur la   Something you use on the beach.
    plage.
30. **calculator:**
    Quelque chose pour faire l'addition,   Something you use to add, subtract, multiply,
    subtraction, multiplication, et division.   and divide.
31. **screwdriver:**
    Quelque chose que tu utilises pour   Something you use to put in nails.
    mettre les clous.
32. **rubber stamp:**
    Il y a d'encre et tu mets sur les papiers.   There is ink and you put it on papers.
33. **rake:**
    Quelque chose que tu utilises pour   Something you use to gather leaves.
    ramasser les feuilles.
34. **drill:**
    Quelque chose que tu utilises pour faire   Something you use to make holes.
    des trous.

35. kettle:
On met si on veut faire du thé ou du café. You take it if you want to make tea or coffee.

36. high-chair:
On met un bébé dedans quand il mange. You put a baby in it when he eats.

37. garden chair:
De fois on le met dehors quand le soleil brille, ou sur la plage. Sometimes you put it outside when the sun shines, or on the beach.

38. wheelchair:
Il y a des roues noires. On assis de sur si tu ne peux pas marcher. It has black wheels. You sit in it if you cannot walk.

39. stroller:
On met un bébé dedans. Il ya des roues noires. You put a baby in it. There are black wheels.

40. swing:
Il y a des fois au parc mais cette fois c'est sur un arbre. They are sometimes in a park, but this time it is in a tree.

41. calculator:
Il y a des nombres et on peut l'utiliser pour multiplier. There are numbers and you can use it to multiply.

42. garden hose:
Quand tu as un jardin et tu veux que le jardin a de l'eau. When you have a garden and you want the garden to have water.

43. paper clamp:
Quand tu as des papiers et tu veux que tu les laisse ensemble. When you have papers and you want them to stay together.

44. potato peeler:
C'est quand tu as un patate et tu veux enlever la peau. It's when you have a potato and you want to take off the skin.

45. wheelchair:
C'est quand quelqu'un ne peut pas marcher et il s'esseoir dans une chaise et ça roule. It's when someone canot walk and he sits in a chair and it rolls.

46. playpen:
C'est quand tu mets un bébé dans comme une petite boite et il joue. It's when you put a baby in like a little box and he plays.

47. drill:
Quand to as une piece de bois et tu veux faire un trou dans le bois. When you have a piece of wood and you want to make a hole in the wood.

48. wrench:
C'est une petite chose en metal. Il y a les deux trous toute en haute et tu l'utilises avec des clous (commes les clous). It's a small metal thing. There are two holes at the top and you use it with nails (like nails).

49. hammer:
Il y a un grand bâton et quelque chose de metal là sur. Et tu frappes des clous. There is a big handle and something metal on it. And you bang nails.

50. shovel:
On utilise pour enlever quelque chose. Tu sauvent utilises dehors ou à la plage. Tu peux faire des trous avec. You use it to lift something. You often use it outside or on the beach. You can make holes with it.

51. garden hose:
C'est quelque chose que l'eau peut sortir de. It's something that water can come out of.

52. paper clamp:
C'est pour mettre des papiers ensembles. It's to keep papers together.

53. wooden spoon:
C'est fait en bois et on l'utilise si on veut faire de gâteau. It's made of wood and you use it if you want to make a cake.

54. swing:
Tu attaches sur un arbre. You attach it to a tree.

55. garden chair:
Si on veut aller dehors et s'asseoir dans   If you want to go outside and sit in the sun.
le soleil.

56. playpen:
C'est quand un bébé veut jouer.   It's when a baby wants to play.

57. stool:
Tu peux s'asseoir.   You can sit on it.

58. paper clamp:
Quand tu veux garder des papiers   When you want to keep papers together, you
ensembles, tu l'utilises.   use it.

59. hammer:
Pour les clous.   For nails.

60. folding-chair:
C'est une autre sorte de chaise.   It's another kind of chair.

61. wagon:
Tu peux mettre des animaux ou des   You can put animals or people in it and you
persones dns et tu le tire.   pull it.

62. beater:
C'est pour si on veut "mixer"   It's for if you want to mix.

63. record player:
Tu mets un "record" sur.   You put a record on it.

64. record player
On peut mettre des disques sur.   You can put records on it

65. can opener:
C'est quand tu as une petite bouteille et   It's when you have a little bottle and there is
il y a une machine et tu veux ouvrir la.   a machine and you want to open it.

66. wing chair:
Quelque chose que tu peux asis dedans.   Something that you can sit in. It's very soft.
C'est très douce.

67. swing:
Quelque chose que tu balance sur.   Something that you can swing on.

68. folding-chair:
Quelque chose que tu assises sur et ça   Something that you can sit in and that can go
peux aller plat. Tu peux le mettre dans   flat. You can put it in your hand and carry it
ta main et la porter quelque part.   anywhere.

69. wrench:
Quand tu as quelque chose qui est   When you have something that is stuck.
"stuck." Quand on a une bouteille du jus   When you have a bottle of juice or
ou quelque chose et puis on veut ouvrir   something and then you want to open the
la petite chose que est sur la bouteille.   little thing that is on the bottle.

70. swing:
C'est une sorte de, tu peux dire, chaise   It's a kind of, you could say, chair for when
que quand tu "move." Des fois c'est sur   you move. Sometimes it is in the trees.
des arbres.

71. child's car seat:
C'est une chaise pur bébé que tu mets   It's a chair for a baby that you put in a car to
dans la voiture pour tu sois "safe' sauf.   keep you safe.
(cf. 16)

72. can opener:
C'est pour les...tu ouvres les...il y a une   It's for the...you open the...There is a magnet.
"magnet."

73. record player:
Tu mets un "record" sur.   You put a record on it.

74. can opener:
C'est un object que tu...tu ouvres des   It's something that you...you open the, tins,
"tins," des boites en metal.   the metal boxes.

QUESTIONS

1.   Consider the previous data. Classify the strategies according to the following categories:
      - paraphrase
      - language switch
      - message abandonment
      - literal translation
      - circumlocution
      - word coinage

2.   Describe the critical feature(s) you used to assign each strategy to a particular category?
      Was there an overlap among categories? Give examples of ambiguous strategies (i.e.,
      strategies that could be classified in more than one category).

3.   What problems did you face in the classification of strategies?

4.   What type of strategy is the most effective from the point of view of communication?

DESCRIPTION AND CLASSIFICATION 2

Native Language: Dutch
Target Language: English
Data Source: Description of geometric shapes
Learner Information:
     Age: Adults, first-year university students in The Netherlands
     Amount of Exposure: Minimum 6 years
     Number of Subjects: 17

METHODOLOGICAL BACKGROUND

All subjects recorded descriptions of each of the 11 shapes given below:

They were told to describe the shapes in such a way that they could be redrawn at a later time by a native speaker. Descriptions were done in Dutch and then one week later in English.

THEORETICAL BACKGROUND

Descriptions can be categorized into three general strategy types:

    1)   **Holistic**
          association of shapes to a "real-world" object or to a known geometric figure
    2)   **Partitive**
          description of a shape as if it were made up of a complex of smaller and simpler shapes
    3)   **Linear**
          breaking shapes up into one-dimensional components

======== **Part One** ========

QUESTIONS

1.   Select any one of the previous shapes and describe them to a partner. Which of the strategy types described (holistic, partitive, linear) did you use? Or, was a combination used?

DATA (numbers in [] refer to picture number)

1. the next form is er...a sort of U upside down [10]
2. The next erm drawing looks like...a letter of the Greek alphabet...the omega...[10]
3. two triangles....their bases are...put together [7]
4. this is a triangle [6]
5. Erm...a P erm...(chuckle) it has, it's not exactly a P, it has a corner...it's not (sigh) [9]
6. Two lines starting in one point...one erm goes to the left side ad the other goes to the...right side erm...and erm......they're about er3 cm long and er...then on top of each of these lines on the left one there is a line which erm starts at the end of er the first line and erm...goes to the right ending in erm one point and on the...right line, on the top of that there's starting another line...er going to the left, and er it ends in the same point as the line I described just er before....[7]
7. the last one is er...erm has a form of a mug [11]
8. then we have some kind of a cross on its side [1]
9. The next picture is er...erm...again four lines...erm equally long...and they are in the form...nee! They are drawn...they two lines bein in erm in erm...point but they come together [7]
10. Simply a square which you find on cards [7]
11. Then you have something er...er...how do you?...it's er a square with er...the corners are not of 90 degrees yo hae er...this...well this is like two triangles...put together,but the line where they are put together has vanished so you have...it's like a "wybertje." (laugh) [7]
    wybertje = brand of diamond shaped licorice lozenges
12. This one is a...erm......erm two triangles...erm 66 to 60 erm degrees angles each...and the one is...erm...their f...their bases are...put together so...erm you have about er er it's a figure like two roofs of a house put together...one going up and one going down like two Vs...one up and w one down...touching each other [7]
13. You make the figure of a licorice with the erm two point opposite each other and then you make in the middle of the...line which you are not(?) don't draw it but imagine it there...opposite that you make two points you make therefore a erm en erm well er of a shape of a....[7]

QUESTIONS

2. Classify the above descriptions as being of one strategy type or another.

3. Which strategy appears to be preferred?

4. Is the preferred strategy from your own description (Part One) the same as the preferred strategy from these nonnative speakers? What explanation can you give for the similarity or difference in approach?

======   **Part Two**   ======

QUESTIONS

5. The following strategy orderings have been attested as individuals attempt to describe the shapes. No other combinations were noted. These orderings are to be interpreted in such a way that the first represents a first attempt and the second (or third) represents successive attempts at a description.

> H
> H, P
> H, L
> H, P, L
> P
> P, L
> L

What is the hierarchical ordering for these three strategy types? What possible explanation is there for this ordering?

*6.   Assuming that the hierarchy in (5) holds cross-linguistically, what implications might
         there be for L2 usage?   In what way could a learner's limited linguistic proficiency affect
         the choice of strategy?

Glossary

Acceptability Judgment: Task in which subjects are asked to assess whether (and/or the extent to which) a given sentence is a possible sentence in a language.

Accessibility Hierarchy: A continuum of relative clause types such that the presence of one type implies the presence of others higher on the hierarchy.

Alveolar: A sound produced with the tip of the tongue raised toward the bony tooth ridge (known as the alveolar ridge).

Approximant: A set of sounds (usually classified as consonants) that has vowel-like qualities (e.g., /r/ and /l/).

Bald-on-record: An interactional strategy in which face threatening is maximized.

Competence: The (mentally represented) linguistic knowledge that underlies speakers' performance in a language.

Comprehension Check: A device used in conversation to ensure that one's interlocutor has understood.

Confirmation Check: A device a speaker uses in conversation to determine if she or he has understood correctly.

Critical Period: The time span from birth to puberty beyond which (according to the Critical Period Hypothesis) successful spontaneous language acquisition cannot take place.

Discourse Completion Task (DCT) A DCT is one in which subjects are provided (usually in writing) with a description of a situation followed by blank lines in which they are to write what they would say in such a situation. In some instances the blank lines are followed by a statement that the respondent would utter. For example, a preliminary description might be "Your professor asks you for a ride home. You say:_____
Professor: "That's too bad. I was really counting on you." The second statement indicates that a refusal is required.

Fossilization: Cessation of learning occurring at any stage before the attainment of native-like linguistic competence.

Interlanguage: The mental grammar constructed, and the language produced, by a nonnative speaker of a language.

Lateral: A sound produced with air flow around the sides of the tongue, like /l/ in English "light."

Magnitude Estimation: Task in which informants are presented with a series of isolated sentences and are instructed to assign any number they wish to the first sentence. This represents that sentence's degree of perceived acceptability. Proportionally higher or lower numbers are then assigned to subsequent sentences according to their degree of perceived acceptability with respect to the first sentence (normally, the higher the number, the more acceptable the sentence). Thus, if a sentence is judged to be twice as acceptable as the previous one, the number assigned to it has to be twice as large; if a sentence is judged to be one-third as acceptable as the previous one, the number assigned will be one-third of the previous one, and so on.

Near-native: A nonnative speaker of a language who is virtually indistinguishable from a native speaker in his or her use of that language.

Negotiation of meaning: The attempt made in conversation to clarify a lack of understanding.

Parameters: Optional values that may be selected by different languages for underlying principles of Universal Grammar; dimensions of language variation.

Performance:	Speakers' actual use of language in concrete situations, affected by underlying linguistic competence as well as by nonlinguistic factors.
Principles:	Abstract linguistic properties of Universal Grammar that are true of all languages.
Retroflex:	A sound produced with the tip of the tongue curled back.
Speech Act:	This refers to what one does with language (i.e., the functions for which language is used). Examples: complaining, complimenting, refusing.
Transfer:	Use of linguistic information from a previously learned language (usually the L1) in the L2.
Universal Grammar:	The set of innate linguistic principles that constitute the abstract form of all human languages; what does not have to be learned by the child on the basis of input.